ALICE *In* SUNDERLAND

ALICE *In* SUNDERLAND

∾ ∾

By
Minerva Spurlock

Printed by CreateSpace 2013
ISBN-13: 978-1480209060
ISBN-10: 1480209066

Library of Congress Control Number: 2012920510
CreateSpace Self Publishing Platform, North Charleston,
South Carolina

Printed in the United States of America City, State

Cover design Artwork by Kimball Gray Davis.
Cover design by Rocky Brewer
This book is printed on acid-free paper.

Acknowledgements

〜

Thank you to all the individuals, professors, and mentors throughout my life who have provided me with an endless supply of inspiration. I find my inspiration comes from the least likely sources, even though I have had my fair share of both positive and negative experiences. I still wear a smile on my face every day thankful for the lessons I have learned and memories I will carry with me for the rest of this lifetime.

Thank you to certain members of my family who have always accepted me the way I am. I am not a typical individual and anyone who has ever met me will vouch for this statement.

I think outside the box and follow my intuition in most cases. I am far from perfect, but at least I have a firm grasp on acceptance, respect, and unconditional love.

Thank you to anyone who has ever cut me down or ridiculed me; your negativity has only fueled my creative, motivational, and inspirational fires. You have assisted me in understanding how the world functions on an ulterior level, and I am thankful for all you have taught me.

Foreword

What you are about to read are my personal journal entries covering the period of time I lived with my great-grandmother. Nothing has been changed except for the names. Throughout my journal, I addressed both my grandmother June, and my great-grandmother Alice, by the name Grams. Now that I have decided to make this personal account public, I thought the interchangeable names might get confusing for readers. I tried to make sure any address or mention of my great-grandmother is by the name Molly, which was her preferred nickname; in like manner, I tried to make sure any address or mention of my grandmother is by the name June. Please know I am only human, and mistakes are inevitable. That is why I am including this key below to help eliminate or at least minimize any confusion.

KEY

My great-grandmother: Alice, Molly, Grams
My grandmother: June, Grandma, Grams
Myself: Jaime, James, Nicks, Minerva, Brewer

One final note: Molly shared some amazing quotes and sayings with me, and I kept track of them all by writing them at the tops of some the journal entry pages. If she shared a good saying or quote, it is written at the top of that particular day's page. I am not sure where all the quotes came from, but they seemed never ending; every other day there was a new saying. I am very thankful I wrote them in my journal, because there is no way I would have remembered them all.

I received a birthday call from my Grandma June on the fourth of December of 2009; she lived in Boise, Idaho at the time. I was living in Portland, Oregon, with my brother and his husband. Grandma June was tired and stressed; I could hear it in her voice.

She told me she had been going to her mother's house twice a day for almost the entire month of October. Once in the mornings—to make sure her mother was getting up, getting dressed, and eating some breakfast. Grandma June would repeat the visit in the early evening. This continued on for about a month until my grandmother made the decision to stop visiting her mother Molly twice a day.

In November, June brought Molly back to her house and attempted to acclimate her to the new living environment. This continued until the first part of December when my great-grandmother's complaining became unbearable. Grandma June took her mother back to her apartment and gave me a call.

I hadn't realized my great-grandmother was doing so poorly. When I say poorly, I mean that in a comparative sense. Poorly for my great-grandmother was actually pretty spectacular. She was on one pill, and that was it as far as medications were concerned. I had seen Molly that previous summer, and she seemed to be doing fine. A little bit slower than what I remembered from Christmas of 2008, but what else do you expect from someone who is ninety-nine years old?

I did not realize until I had the phone conversation with my grandma June at the first part of December, that my great-grandma was is need of some assistance getting dressed. That surprised me; I guess I figured she was like the Energizer Bunny™. The harsh reality set in that she was slowly winding down. I could hear it in my grandmother's voice, the sadness, the frustration, the anger, and the helplessness. My nurturing instincts immediately kicked in, and I agreed to move to Boise and help out.

Over the next couple days, I was on the phone quite a bit with my grandmother, trying to make the best decisions for my great-grandmother. After discussing the nursing home option and the option to bring Molly back to live at June's, we came to a decision. We decided to do whatever was best for great-grandma, which meant for me to move in with her. We decided I would move in so I could be available throughout the night in case Molly needed anything or had any accidents.

We discussed the harsh reality of the situation, which was the fact Molly was getting older. June and I were both thankful that Molly was happy, healthy, and free from pains. What more can you ask at that age?

Grandma June called the resident complex where her mother lived and spoke with the manager, Lorie. She explained the situation and asked if I could move in with my great-grandmother to be a live-in and assist her. Lorie and the entire building welcomed me with open arms, and I will always be grateful for that. Lorie made me copies of the keys, showed me around, and welcomed me with a big potluck dinner a few nights after I moved in to thank me for coming to help their dear and beloved friend, Molly.

Once June and I had the OK from Lorie to move in, I began packing up my things. My brother Rocky and his husband Kimball said they would take care of my cats while I was gone, and I headed to Boise, Idaho for my new adventure.

To Grandma Molly,
Thank you for the incredible memories.

December 21, 2009
Monday

I packed up the '69 Chevelle and drove from Portland to Boise a few days ago. I arrived at Grandma Molly's and unpacked my suitcase. Grandma June had cleared out the bottom drawer of the dresser in the hallway for me, so that was nice. My few items fit nice and comfortably in the bottom drawer. Because Molly's apartment is a one bedroom, she is obviously set up to sleep in the bedroom.

June and I decided the least invasive thing for me to do was to set up a day bed in the living room. The east-facing wall is lined with the windows and the west-facing wall has the opening that leads to the bedroom, entryway, and kitchen. The south-facing wall has Molly's sunflower couch against it with the coffee table in front of the couch. The north-facing wall had the television backed up to it, but I moved it so it was in the northeastern corner of the room. I think it will work out well because the daybed can be disguised as a couch in the daytime, and I can sleep on it through the night. The bonus is that the television stand has shelves on the sides of it for DVDs. Not that I watch DVDs, but I do read, so I have my books on the television stand that is right next to the day bed now. Sweet.

Tonight is my first night staying with Grandma Molly. We will see how things go. It is nine o'clock, and she just went to bed.

~Minerva

December 22, 2009
Tuesday

I assisted Molly with taking a shower for the first time today. This was a big project; I could tell she was not comfortable with me helping her undress and bathe. She kept telling me she could bathe later because she wasn't dirty. I told her it had to be done because hygiene is super-important in case her friends stop by the apartment to visit. With the thought planted in her mind that random people may stop by unannounced, she agreed to both the bathing and the assistance.

I was a little curious as to how she would do getting into the bathtub. It is one of the standard bathtub/shower combos. I was concerned about her having to step over the tub wall into the slippery bottom of the tub.

We picked out what she wanted to wear after her shower, and I turned on the water. I laid down a huge towel in the bottom of the shower for her to stand on—just like I do for my kitties when I don't feel like having them slide all across the bottom of the shower tub. We turned on the heat lamp in the bathroom, and then I helped her get undressed. She held on to the handrails, and I kept my hands near her back just in case she needed me. She did not though; she got in without any assistance.

Molly hung on to the rails and stepped into the tub by herself. I gave her a quick wash and then shut off the water. I dried her off, and then she stepped out of the tub onto a towel I had laid on the floor for non-slip, gripping purposes. I grabbed the clothes she had picked out, and I helped her get dressed.

What a monumental moment in our relationship. I am so happy she is feeling comfortable with me. All I want is for her to feel comfortable.

On a side note, the temperature is outrageous in this apartment. One, it has to be eighty-five degrees in Molly's place—I slept in a t-shirt and my panties—and without covers. I couldn't handle the heat.

Two, I lay on my little day bed trying to fall asleep. I felt like Sylar from Heroes was in the room. Molly has four different clocks that I can distinguish from one another while lying there in the dark. Each one has a different tick—it is unbelievable.

One goes: tick, tick, tick, tick.
Another goes: tick, tick, pause, tick, tick, pause.
Another goes: tick, pause, tick, pause.
Another goes: tick, chink, pause, tick, chink, pause.

I finally fell asleep and slept very well. One full day down, not bad at all.

~*Minerva*

Day two with Molly. Molly is doing well. She woke up about ten o'clock this morning, and we got dressed and had some breakfast. We walked around the halls a bit, had some tea, ate our lunch, and, of course, had some more tea. We watched the Canadian geese out the window for a bit and then went down to the common area to visit with June. She had stopped by to see how things were going. I took a couple of pictures, and then Grandma June left for the day.

I played the piano for Molly for about fifteen minutes, and then she introduced me to her favorite past time: judging people who walk by. It is not just the people coming into the building who receive and fall victim to criticism, condemnation, and denunciation of various sorts; it's the people leaving as well. It was quite an unbelievable and entertaining afternoon to say the least. We eventually meandered back upstairs for some more tea, and Molly went to sleep around nine o'clock again.

Molly woke up around eleven o'clock. I could hear her rustling about in her room. I was about to get up to go check on her; I wanted to make sure she was okay. I heard her walker moving, so I stayed put for the time being. There was a single nightlight shedding soft light from the bathroom directly across the hall from her bedroom. I knew she couldn't see me super well all the way across the living room, so I pretended to be asleep when she came out of her room. I had my eye lids cracked just enough to see her when she came into the hall, looked around the corner, and stopped.

She was just staring at me; she reminded me of Bill Cosby when he does his Johnny Bench impersonation.

She slowly started to walk toward me. First, she would move her walker out in front of her, and then she would move her feet closer to the walker. I continued to pretend I was unconscious. She continued getting closer until she reached the end of the daybed down by my feet. She stared again for about ten to fifteen seconds. Then she continued walking along the side of the bed until she was right next to my face.

I won't lie; my heart was pounding in my chest. I was scared. I don't know why. I am not sure what I thought was going to happen, but the whole chain of events just seemed too bizarre and weird to me.

At this point Molly's body was about a foot away from my face. She leaned down and put her face within inches of mine. At that point I had to close my eyes. I thought I was going to laugh out loud and give her a heart attack for sure. I kept my composure though. After about thirty seconds, she leaned upright and walked back to her bedroom. She shut the light off and went to sleep.

Good times at Grandma Molly's.

~Minerva

Christmas Eve
Thursday

Day three with Molly. One of the clocks broke last night—so it is a little quieter—thank goodness. Molly gave me great advice today.

"He who expecteth nothing
is never disappointed."

~Alice

Then Molly asked me if I wanted to get married. I laughed and said, "No, not really."

She continued to tell me "Mr. Right" would find me while I was busy not looking for him. She really is sweet. I love her with all my heart. I am thankful I was given this opportunity to spend time with her. I am thankful my circumstances allowed for me to come back from Portland and help her out.

She was born in 1910; I can't even imagine everything she has gone through. I do know that I would never want her to be placed in a nursing home. I am not saying every home for the elderly is horrible; I am saying removing Grandma Molly from this apartment was not an option for me.

I don't know the first thing about the individuals who are placed in nursing homes. I do know I am an extremely rational human being, and I realize my reasoning may be a downfall at times. Removing Molly from a place where she has lived and been accustomed to for the past forty years does not seem rational or logical to me. She knows this place. She loves this place. I am not a doctor or a nurse, but I can tell you I honestly believe moving Molly would be traumatic and detrimental to her well being.

So I am here for the long haul—however long that may be. Protecting Molly, doing what I think is best for her, and loving her the only way I know how.

~Minerva

December 25, 2009
Christmas Day
Friday

"Choke up chicken."

~Alice

I took Molly up to June's today for Christmas. June had invited us up to her place to spend the afternoon. The three of us ate chicken, potatoes, stuffing, cranberries, and green beans. Dinner was simple and tasty—just the way I like it.

While Molly was in the care of June, I ran over to Mom and Dad's because it is literally seventeen houses down the street. I hung out with Mom and Dad from about noon until one o'clock. I saw Aunt Charlie, George, Jenna, and Evelyn; they were all spending time with Mom and Dad for the holidays. It was so great to have a small family gathering. After experiencing some of the family reunions we had growing up, you begin to appreciate the smaller gatherings.

I am pretty excited to be back in Boise. I can spend time with Mom, Dad, and my grandmas.

~Nicks

December 26, 2009

Saturday

THE DIRTY UNDERWEAR GANG:

Arguably the best part of *Young Guns* is when they discuss a gang consisting of members with dirty underwear. Or is it that you make other people's underwear dirty by scaring the bejesus out of them?

Either way, I am bringing it back. Here comes 2010—the year of the dirty underwear gang.

By the way, random side note and question: Where did the word "bejesus" come from? It is such a weird word. And speaking of Jesus, I have this question that keeps formulating in my mind when he is brought up. I have heard people exclaim "Jesus H. Christ." Does anyone know what the "H" stands for? My best guess is the "H" stands for Jesus...in the Hispanic pronunciation, not the English. When you pronounce Jesus in Spanish, it sounds like it would start with an "H" sound, i.e., "Hay-Zeus."

~Minerva

14

December 27, 2009
Sunday

I went for a drive tonight—I wanted to see the city lights at night from Table Rock. I remember wanting to see the sunrise from there so bad. If I get the chance, I may do that while I am back in Boise.

Molly runs on a pretty consistent routine from what I am finding out. She wakes up around nine o'clock and heads to the restroom. After that, I help her get dressed unless it is a day I help her bathe. If it is a day I help her shower, we obviously do the cleaning before we get dressed.

Then we have some tea and visit while I cook breakfast. Sometimes she likes to sit in her comfortable, poofy chair. I move it after breakfast over to the window; so now it's as close as one can get to the windowsill...she loves it, though. So sometimes she sits in her chair and checks on the world, giving me frequent updates as to what everyone is doing.

The other times she sits at the kitchen table because it is right across the counter from where I do the cooking. I always ask Molly what she would like for breakfast, and she tends to want one of three things: pancakes and eggs, cornbread and muffins, or biscuits and sausage gravy. This morning she wanted cornbread and muffins.

On with her routine: after breakfast she likes to watch out the window for a little while, making sure no one is doing things she wouldn't approve of.

Around eleven o'clock we head out for a walk. The destination and duration of the walks vary, but they will continue to be a part of the routine for as long as she is able. Around noon we have another cup of tea and wait for lunch to arrive. It usually shows up between noon and quarter after. Before I arrived in Boise, June had it set up so the Meals-on-Wheels people would bring her mother a meal every day for lunch. She wanted to make sure her mother always had something to eat, and winters around Boise are sometimes unpredictable. June never wanted to be in a position where she couldn't get down to the apartment complex to help her mother eat. The meals vary, and Molly seems to like them. She eats half for lunch and half for dinner. As long as she is happy with that, I will be too.

After lunch, we enjoy another cup of tea and check on the world—to make sure everyone is behaving themselves.

In the afternoon, Molly and I venture back downstairs to the main lobby area to people watch. We watch the people coming and going, and let me tell you, Molly has something to say about every single one of them. She is a walking factoid generator. She knows something about everyone— and not just the usual boring birthday dates. I am talking she knows whose grandchild is sleeping with the gardener and which children are leaving their husbands or wives. She knows who brings the same dishes to the potlucks time after time, and she knows just about where everyone is going or coming from.

I sometimes play the piano while we are down there; I do enjoy being able to provide some entertainment for the cute people who live in that building. Today I had a gentleman who came up and introduced himself as Howard. He told me his friends call him Howie. He asked me if I could play, "My Heart Will Go On." I told him I didn't know it off the top of my head but to give me a few minutes. Sure enough, I had it figured out in about five minutes. Howie was so happy to hear that song. He was sitting on the couch next to Molly, and he was crying—it was really sweet. I could hear him singing along.

So after Molly and I do the people watching/ piano playing routine downstairs, we head back up to her apartment for some more tea. We visit, and I ask her questions about the past and the experiences I know she has burned into her long-term memory. She seems to be happy to share the stories, and I am videotaping some of them.

Around five o'clock we have dinner, which consists of Meals-on-Wheels for her, and whatever I decide to have. I have been in the mood for apples and kidney beans lately. After dinner, we get into our pajamas, have some more tea, and visit while watching the world from her poofy chair. Technically she occupies her poofy chair, and I sit on the floor or in a different chair. She tends to get tired between eight and nine o'clock and I help her into bed.

~Minerva

December 28, 2009
Monday

"I am not as green as I am cabbage."
~Alice

Apparently the Idaho State government and possibly the Federal government don't have enough important things to do with their time. Grandma June told me they were questioning my great-grandmother and her citizenship. It is hard to believe that the government wants to deport a ninety-nine-year-old woman back to Canada. I know my great-grandmother moved from England to Canada shortly after World War II. Around the year 1948, my great-grandmother brought her second husband, Mac, and her only daughter, June, to Canada. Grandma June was about seventeen at the time.

I know Molly worked in Canada for a while and then moved to the United States with the family at some point in the late '50s.

So back to modern day, Grandma June called me and needed my help contacting the social security administration. The goal was to obtain a copy of my great-grandmother's social security card. She had been working and paying taxes since the late '50s. The whole thing seemed like a waste of time.

So I pulled up Google maps on the Internet and typed in:

Boise, Idaho, Social Security Administration

The search resulted in about twenty different numbers and locations. I picked one and called 208.334.1403.

Here is the conversation that took place a couple of hours ago:

Him: Hello?

Me: Umm—is this not a certain business?

Him: How did you get this number?

Me: Well, how about never mind, and this is obviously the wrong number.

I hung up the phone and proceeded to select a different and hopefully the correct number for the social security administration office. Before I could dial the new number, the number I had just hung up on, called me back. I recognized the number on my caller ID screen.

Me: Hello?

Him: Who is this?

Me: What? Who is this?

Him: This is the US Secret Service. In fact, this is a secure and private line. Now, please tell me where you got the number.

Me: Yeah, right! If you really are the Secret Service, I am sure you will have no problem figuring out who I am.

I was totally laughing, out loud, at the man on the phone. I hung up on him again. I am thinking it was someone like me, who would totally say that kind of thing. Brilliant actually—I am going to change my voicemail to have something do to with the Secret Service.

~Minerva

I met Grandma June at what she likes to call the "Mandralin Palace." She has been a part of a bridge group that meets there every Monday mornings at eleven thirty. They eat something and then play a few rounds of bridge. Is it rounds or hands? I need to learn these things before I accidentally offend someone. I told June I would meet her there some Mondays and visit with her and her friends while everyone is eating.

I did not really want anything to eat from there after hearing what a friend of mine saw. Apparently, this particular electrician took a rewiring job at the Mandarin Palace. While he was in the kitchen rewiring their sockets and light switches, he found dead mice and rats. He also found ants on the counters. Really, though—that is why I hate eating out.

Speaking of eating out...I love those movies.

Eating Out 3—my favorite; *Eating Out 1*—my second favorite; *Eating Out: 2*—my least favorite.

I told all the ladies in June's bridge group about the Secret Service/wrong number debacle. They were totally laughing. Mary Margaret told me to hook up with a member of the secret service because she has dealt with them before, and they are all good looking. Wow on the stereotypes, that cracks me up.

~Minerva

"We have nothing to do,
and all day to do it."

~Alice

This afternoon about four o'clock someone knocked on Molly's door. I looked through the peephole and could not believe my eyes. I opened the door to three men in black suits.

Him: You must be Jaime Brewer.

Me: Seriously?

Him: Yes, ma'am. We ran the number on the call we received yesterday through our data base system. We then traced this number through GPS and tracked its location.

Me: You spent tax dollars on that?

Him: Ma'am, I need you to tell me where you got that number.

Me: It came up on Google maps while I was doing a search for social security offices in Boise, Idaho.

Him: I need you to show me, ma'am.

I did show him on my laptop, and he was angry—but not at me, thank God. He was about forty, extremely good-looking, and, I am thinking, somewhat narcissistic. He told his friends or partners, whatever you want to call them, to go down and wait by the elevators. He apologized for being so forceful with his questioning and implied the importance of that number being kept secure. He made me delete the number out of my phone as he watched. He then asked me if I wanted to grab a cup of coffee with him sometime.

I politely declined the offer, and he left. What a crazy day! The US Secret Service tracks me down in Boise, Idaho, for a mistake on Google maps. The Secret Service in Boise, Idaho, actually came and talked to me today because I called a wrong number. Why is there a secret service agent in Boise, Idaho? Are we that cool or that dangerous?

Isn't that ironic? Don't you think?

~Minerva

December 30, 2009
Wednesday

"All dolled up like a dog's tail."

~Alice

Molly and I had a great conversation today; we were discussing the topic of regret. I asked her if she regretted anything, and if so, what. The first thing that came out of her mouth, without hesitation, was the fact she had wanted to be a lawyer. She told me she regretted the fact that she didn't pursue her dreams. She told me that women were laughed at back in her day if they even mentioned wanting to do a job that was designated for men. I found the entire conversation to be so fascinating.

I asked her if she regretted anything else, and the next thing she regretted was a decision she made back at the beginning of World War II. Because of her decision, the relationship between her and her daughter, June, suffered immensely. She talked about the war again and the entire process of her making the decision to send June inland.

The reasoning behind sending the children who lived in coastal England to inland locations was to decrease the chances of them being bombed by Germany. Molly said it was the hardest decision she ever had to make, and she regrets the fact she chose to drive ambulances and assist military forces throughout the course of the war instead of choosing to be with her daughter.

1940 St. John's Ambulance Brigade.
Molly is second from the right.

1942. St. John's Ambulance Brigade.

She said she knows that decision caused June to despise her for the rest of their lives. I tried to not tear up while Grandma Molly was talking, but I had never heard her open up as she did today. I am so glad I asked the question.

~Nicks

RHUBARB PEACH PIE WITH A CRUNCHY MACAROON TOPPING

- Preheat oven to 375 degrees.
- Mix together flour, sugars, nutmeg, and salt in a bowl. In a larger bowl, beat the egg and orange juice together. Add rhubarb, peaches, and zest. Sprinkle dry ingredients over top and toss gently.
- Pour the filling into the piecrust.
- Sprinkle with topping. Bake on bottom one-third of the oven for an hour.

TOPPING:

2 1/2 cups crumbled coconut macaroons

3/4-cup whole pecans

1/4 cup brown sugar

6 Tbsp. cold butter cut into 1/4" cubes

- Mix all topping ingredients together until it forms a coarse meal

INGREDIENTS:

5 Tbsp. flour

3/4-cup sugar

1/4 cup brown sugar

1/4 tsp. nutmeg

1/2 tsp. salt

1 egg

1 orange, zested and juiced

14 ozs. Chopped rhubarb

12 ozs. peeled, sliced peaches

Still New Year's Eve

"You've got to give——to get."

~Alice

Molly and I partied downstairs in the common room with the rest of the residents from her building, who were all celebrating New Year's Eve. We showed up around six thirty and stayed until Molly got tired, which was around nine thirty. Because Molly doesn't weigh very much, I try to get her to eat whenever I can. She did great and munched on cookies, cupcakes, and brownies pretty much the entire time we were downstairs at the party.

I met Mary Mann, who lives in 4102. She looks like Dolly Parton. I also met Richard Shaw, who lives in 4412. He is a handsome older gentleman who looks like an old-school cowboy. Hell, he was probably the Marlboro man.

Molly and I finally went back upstairs to her apartment, and I helped her change into her nightgown. She gets upset if I call them her pajamas. She always tells me ladies wear nightgowns. After the wardrobe change, I helped Molly get into bed.

I then picked up Chad, and we headed to Grandma Evelyn's house. Evelyn is my Mom's mother—June is my Dad's mom. I visited with Grandma Evelyn for about half an hour and reminisced about the time back in 1992 when we spent New Year's together. My younger brother Rocky and I heard Grandma Evelyn was going to be in the hospital over New Year's so we decided to go down and ring in the new year with her. I was fourteen, and my brother was eleven. Between the approximate hours of eight-thirty and midnight, my brother and I made several trips from Grandma Evelyn's hospital room, to different vending machines, located on various floors.

We started out playing Pictionary on the nurse's whiteboard in Grandma Evelyn's hospital room. It was lucky the nurses had left us the dry erase markers along the bottom ledge of the white board. But honestly, knowing vending machine food was nearby was too much of a distraction. Food seemed so mysterious and extra yummy coming out of a machine. The machines seemed to be strategically placed throughout the hospital.

Over the short course of about three hours, I managed to down about half a dozen egg salad sandwiches, three or four tuna sandwiches, four or five Milky Ways®, at least three Reese's Peanut Butter Cups®, a bag of the red Skittles®, and a couple packs of Rolos®. It was during the infamous Dick-Clark-is-in-Times-Square-and-everyone-around-the-country-is-watching-the-ball-drop, that disaster struck. It was thanks to those final seconds of that particular year, that a nightmare of a memory exists. During the final seconds of 1992, I ran for the hospital room bathroom. I remember everyone on TV yelling, cheering, and celebrating the new year. It wasn't just on the television: Nurses, doctors, and patients, there in the hospital were also cheering on all the New Year's resolutions they knew fully well they had no intentions of keeping.

As I knelt, hovering above the toilet bowl, vomiting all the deliciousness I had previously downed, I remember thinking what a waste of marvelous food. What a horrible and disgusting way to ring in the new year.

Back to present day. Aunt Charlie and my cousin Madison were also at Grandma Evelyn's. I took Evelyn a copy of *The Devil Wears Prada*. I put the movie on, I visited with Madison for a few, and then Chad and I left. We visited my Mom and Dad's after that. We basically said hi, dropped off some food, grabbed one of my glow sticks from my caving supplies, and then headed back to Chad's.

Chad lives with his younger brother Jason. Jason had a group of friends over and they had apparently been ringing in the new year together. I activated the glow stick, cut it open, and flung it all over in the living room. It was so hard not to laugh. There were four people sleeping in the living room when we got there—or maybe they were passed out. Either way, there were glow stick juice sprinkles all over the people, the couches, the walls, and the ceiling. No one noticed except for Chad and me.

Happy New Year! I said good night to Chad and headed back to Molly's. I checked on Molly; she was sound asleep. So I too entertained the notion. I crawled into bed and fell asleep as well.

~Nicks

January 1, 2010
Friday

"People always want more;
they are never satisfied."

~Alice

Molly had a checkup with the doctor today. We got dressed, ate some French toast, and then proceeded to drive over to the hospital for her appointment.

Today the doctor informed me that I needed to put more weight on Molly. This is the same concern he had a couple months ago when Molly and June came in for a checkup. I had been following the doctor's orders since day one of my arrival. Molly does not eat a large amount to begin with, so I have to focus on the quality rather than the quantity. I have been feeding her all kinds of nutrient and calorie-dense foods including the fantastic French toast breakfast I made her this morning. It was complete with grenadine syrup.

After the doctor's appointment, we headed to June's. We hung out with June for most of the day. We ate spaghetti for dinner, and I made that peach-rhubarb pie thingy because Molly absolutely loves it. We played some cards and visited. I took Molly home around seven o'clock and helped her change into her nightgown. I made us a cup of tea, and we chatted about her past. She was telling me about driving the ambulance in the war, and how important her job was.

1941 St. John's Ambulance Brigade.

Molly is in the top right corner, sitting on top of the ambulance. Around nine o'clock I helped Molly get into bed, and then I crawled into bed myself. It was a great day. About two, Molly got up to use the restroom. I hopped up as I always do just to make sure she didn't need any assistance from me. She looked great heading into the bathroom, but it looked as if she didn't pull her nightgown all the way up to her waist. As a result, she urinated on her nightgown. I knocked on the bathroom door that was halfway open. She told me to hang on a minute because she was in there. I waited for her to finish, and once she went over to the sink and turned on the faucet to wash her hands, I went in. I did my best to make light of the situation. I was really trying to make sure she didn't feel embarrassed. I told her it looked as if the nightgown got in the way, and she laughed, agreeing with me. I told her to hang tight and I was going to grab a fresh, clean one for her. We got her cleaned up, changed, and back into bed. She held my hand for a minute and had the biggest smile on her face. She told me I was an angel, and that my Grandfather and Dad were both extremely proud of me.

~*Minerva*

January 2, 2010
Saturday

"You die if you worry.You die if you don't,
So why worry at all?"

~Alice

Molly gave me this advice while we were eating breakfast this morning. She has some of the greatest words of wisdom. I did her nails today before we ate breakfast. Now there is less of a chance of feces getting underneath her fingernails.

I have been noticing a problem with Molly these past couple days. I notice she is not wiping herself as well as she used to. She will come out from the bathroom about half the time and have feces underneath her fingernails. I have just been popping over to her as she comes out of the bathroom and making sure her nails are clean. If they are not, I happily remind her she needs to wash her hands. She lets me help her whenever I ask. I use the nail scrubby brushy thing, but I finally decided to cut her nails down short to help with the problem. I don't mind scrubbing her nails every day, but her skin seems so soft and frail, so I think eliminating part of the problem is a good idea. So Saturdays are now designated salon days for us—every Saturday I will give her a manicure and a pedicure.

She still wipes fine: She wipes from front to back, and she is not soiling herself. I think it must be the initial wipes where she is getting the feces under her nails. I have seen her sitting on the toilet using the toilet paper to try and clean her fingers off, so she still is coherent enough to understand that the feces should not be there. While she is on the toilet, she will take toilet paper off the roll and rip it along the perforated lines. She takes the individual squares and lines them up on the bathroom counter, which is on her left. She gets about ten squares lined up and then leaves them there for the next time she comes in to go to the bathroom. When she gets down to one or two remaining squares, she starts her toilet paper prepping project again.

~Minerva

> *"Damn kids come looking for*
> *you when they need money."*
>
> ~*Alice*

I bought Molly some new pajamas today…I mean nightgowns.

They are so cute, and they are two pieces so she won't have such a hard time going to the bathroom during the night. These past couple of days, I have noticed Molly wetting herself while going to the bathroom at night. I figured it out. She is discombobulated in the middle of the night, so she does not pull up her nightgown all the way and ends up urinating on it.

I always get up in the night when Molly goes to the bathroom, because I don't want her going to bed in a wet nightgown or with feces on her hands. I have noticed her nightgown getting wet for the past couple of nights. She has been telling me she does not know when it happens, but I can tell from the look on her face that is not the case. It is simply pride; no one wants to admit that they are losing control of themselves. So I make light of the situation and help Molly change and get into a clean nightgown.

I think I am a pretty good problem solver. I am hoping with the two-piece nightgown, she will have fewer issues going to the bathroom. Pulling a nightgown up to go to the bathroom is opposite of her daily routine of pulling down her pants. I hope that by giving her the ability to pull her nightgown down, it will help make her nighttime trips to the restroom a bit cleaner. Time will tell.

~Minerva

"Life is what you make it."

~Alice

Commodities were delivered today. There had been fliers up around Molly's building by the mailboxes, near the elevators, and on the community bulletin board. The sign said to come down to the manager's office at eleven o'clock to pick up the commodities. Molly and I got down to the manager's office at just before eleven, and there were none. The lady in charge of handing out the commodity rations told me the housing committee delivered twenty-four portions—even though thirty-three people filled out the proper forms and signed up on the official register. The lady informed me they handed out the available portions they did have at ten thirty. I was really upset by that. I called Dee, the woman in charge of the entire program. I talked with her for a while, and she apologized. She told me she would send out the remaining rations on Wednesday, at nine thirty.

I have been watching the *Ten Commandments* with Charlton Heston and Yul Brynner...I think the film is from 1951. I didn't realize what a good-looking guy Heston was. And to tell you the truth, I would have watched it a long time ago if I had known Yul Brynner was in it. Okay, that is probably a lie, but to be fair—my, my, what a good-looking man. The entire movie is great as a whole. The story—the production— quite amazing work for a movie put together so long ago. I just ignore the fact it is a Bible story and understand it to be fiction.

~Minerva

January 5, 2010
Tuesday

*"The single most important ingredient
of human beauty is intelligence."*

~*Minerva*

*"The only thing I have no tolerance for
in this world is ignorance."*

~*Minerva*

I have been reading through one of the IF books for the past couple nights—there are some great questions in there. If I could find out one work of fiction was actually true—it would have to be something ridiculous and far out there like, Stephen King's *The Stand*.

Today was a noticeable glitch in Molly's memory system. She was using the restroom and hollered for me. I went in to make sure she was okay, and she looked rather upset. She was confused because all the toilet paper squares she had laid out for herself were now gone. This is the first time this has happened; she does not remember the fact that she is the one using up the toilet paper. She asked me where all the toilet paper squares she set out had disappeared to. I told her the first thing that came to my mind. I told her Harry Potter had come over during the night and had a bathroom emergency. I suggested perhaps Harry Potter used the toilet paper and had forgotten to replace it. She was not happy about the idea of Harry Potter using her bathroom or her toilet paper.

When she came out of the bathroom, she said, "Tell me more about Mr. Potter." The best part is, she has an English accent so it sounds more authentic. I told her he lived in the building somewhere, I wasn't sure of the exact floor or room number. She informed me she was going to be keeping an eye on her toilet paper from now on to make sure Mr. Potter didn't use it all up again.

That's a good thing; it gives her something to do.

~*Minerva*

January 6, 2010
Wednesday

"Great life if you don't weaken."

~Alice

Molly says this a few times a day—actually she sings it—and then I sing back, "So we're not going to weaken!"

It cracks me up. Molly and I will be walking into the grocery store, and she will start singing that song and people, without fail, smile if they hear her. I am having such a great time with Molly. I can't wait to get her "High School Musical" bedding. I told her about new bedding this morning, and she is all for it. I told her we should get her some new sheets, and I knew where to purchase the perfect sheets for her.

Molly is always in good spirits, and I think her entire attitude is really helping her situation. She is so happy about everything. She is always laughing at something, and she is still so talkative. We went to the doctor's this morning, and he said she is doing fantastic. He said to let her eat whatever she wants to eat, because we want to keep weight on her. She is five feet one inch tall and weighed in at eighty-nine pounds today, which is three pounds up from her December weigh-in.

~Minerva

January 7, 2010
Thursday

"Laugh and the world laughs with you,
cry and you cry alone."

~Alice

Molly is always and forever making me laugh. She does this thing in the store, or walking down the hall, where she says, "Pip pip." It means get moving, or move along, depending on the context. It is so funny when she does it, though.

Molly and I walk every day. Sometimes I can get her outside, and we drive over to the grocery store to walk around. Sometimes it is down the hall and back a few times. Sometimes it is down the hall, into the elevators, and around the common area. Sometimes it is to the mailbox. There is the piano down in the common area, and sometimes she asks me to play stuff for her. Some days we go for drives and walk around random grocery stores, like WinCo or Fred Meyer's, and other days we just hang around the building. I don't care where we go, I just try to keep her moving for two reasons. The first reason is so her muscles continue functioning to the best of their ability. If they stop working out, they get weaker; and if she gets weaker, then she doesn't want to walk around. The second reason is so she doesn't just sit at home all day. She seems to want to sit at home—unless I suggest a walk to the common room, an adventure to the grocery store, or a trip up to visit June. In between our walks, we of course have to refuel and rehydrate ourselves with plenty of tea and biscuits. We have, on average, six cups of tea per day. I am beginning to wonder if all this tea consumption is just an excuse to eat some cookies.

~Minerva

January 7, 2010
Still Thursday

Books I want to get:

-*Invisible Cities* by Italo Calvino
-*Straw Dogs: Thoughts on Humans & Other Animals* by
John Gray
-*The God Delusion* by Richard Dawkins
-*Behold a Pale Horse* by Milton William Cooper
-*Why I Am Not Christian* by Bertrand Russell
-*Discourses* by Epictetus
-*Reading Maketh a Full Man* by Francis Bacon
-*Protocols of the Wise Men of Zion*
-*The Assault on Reason*
-*Religion Explained*
-*God: The Failed Hypothesis, How Science Shows God
Does-Not-Exist*
-*Letter To a Christian Nation*
-*The End of Faith; Religion, Terror, and the Future of
Reason*
-*Kingdom Coming; The Rise of Christian Nationalism*
-*The Concluding Unscientific Postscript* by Soren
Kierkegaard

January 8, 2010
Friday

"Dressed up like a duck ready to be eaten."
~Alice

That is one of the funniest ones I've heard yet. What does that even mean? I mean, I get it—but really—who says that? I was getting ready to go grab a bite to eat with Chad. I was putting on my shoes, and that flew out of her mouth. I laughed so hard. She asked me if I wanted some money for my "date" and then tried to give me two dollars. Oh my god, that is the best, I am going to remember that forever.

I returned back to Molly's place around seven thirty that evening. She was sitting in her comforter, sipping on some tea, munching on some biscuits, and watching traffic out her window. Her living room windows face east, so we get to look out at the corner of 13th and River Street. Molly is on the fourth floor, which is also nice because we can see further around the neighborhood. It seems there is always something to watch outside her window; it is great entertainment.

When you look out the living room window, there is a huge, unmaintained, vacant lot right across the street. It is composed of dirt, grass, and a few trees. The property is probably close to two acres in size, and it is right on the corner of River and South 13th.

If I look to the right of the vacant lot, there is a small, two-story, Victorian-style house, zoned for commercial business. They offer haircuts and other salon services. Next to the house is the post office, and next to the post office is the Boise River. It takes me about forty-five seconds to reach the river from the front door of Molly's building.

So this evening when I came home, she was watching a herd of deer that had come to feed on grass in the empty lot. There were about a dozen of them; they were white tails, and they were so beautiful.

I made myself a cup of tea and visited with Molly while we watched the deer. She told me she was sorry I didn't get to spend more time with her while I was growing up. I told her not to worry about it, and I told her I was so happy that she let me move in with her. We were both having a great time and enjoying each other's company.

~*Minerva*

January 9, 2010
Saturday

"I am putting on weight like nobody's business."
~Alice

Molly told me today that Grandma June is a spoiled brat. I was giving her a pedicure and just getting ready to put on the red polish she had picked out. I asked her if she could elaborate on one of her sayings, which is:

"Your grandmother is spoiled.
June can be whatever she wants to be."

I asked her what Grandma June wants to be. She told me Grandma June wants to be first all the time. Molly told me her daughter is selfish and always puts her self first. Molly said, "She puts herself first before you. She puts herself before me. She puts herself before everyone."

I fell off the chair I was laughing so hard.

~Minerva

"I don't know what I don't know."

~Alice

Every step I take—I look twice. Every decision I make—I pause. I throw caution to the wind. Not for fear, not for guilt, not for comfort.

There can be peace in the unknown, in the uncertainty. There is a stillness upon my heart, like a calm in the open sea. What we share is rare, beautiful, peaceful, and alluring. Pursuing happiness for me is pursuing another woman's livelihood. I am attempting to steer her boat because the captain has jumped overboard.

She is all there sometimes, and I can primarily tell that when we have our talks. She addresses me as her granddaughter, and she tells me she appreciates my loving assistance. Other times though, I can tell she is slipping. If for only sporadic moments here and there, it seems the inevitable has started to present itself. I live everyday with her; thankful this bonding opportunity presented itself. I can tell she gets extremely frustrated when she forgets things; I cannot yet tell if that behavior is in reaction to embarrassment, confusion, or perhaps a combination of each.

I think the best thing for me to do, and the action that feels right, is not to correct her when she forgets something. June tried correcting her earlier today about who I was. While we were up at June's, I went to the bathroom.

During this time, Molly told her daughter how wonderful it was to have the nice nurse lady living with her. I heard what was going on as I came out of the bathroom. June was trying to correct her mother on the faulty assumption. June was trying to explain to Molly that I was her great-granddaughter. I stood behind Molly shaking my head at June, trying to get her to stop. I could see it in Molly's eyes when I came out of the bathroom—she was sincerely confused and thought her daughter was mistaken.

So I took Molly home, and by the time we arrived back at her place, she was back to calling me her granddaughter. I made us some tea, and we watched the world out the window, while chatting about people who live here in the building.

Misdirection leads to honesty—sarcasm leads to happiness. Simplicity in its truest form goes unnoticed by the common eye. To myself—knowing what to look for—knowing the signs—going with my gut instincts. Time is never wasted, only cherished and accepted for what it truly is.

Hiding amongst the bitterroot branches, I see the flame of brutality working its wicked randomness. My heart is aflutter for the spontaneity it is fed. One bite at a time, one blink at a time, one day at a time—I am absolute.

I found this picture of Molly and me; it was taken in 2004 at Sandy's, who is Molly's granddaughter. We are laughing because she is playing with a saltshaker shaped as a little hula dancer. I can definitely vouch for humor as being inherited.

~Nicks

"I believe you…thousands wouldn't."

~*Alice*

That has to be one of the funniest things I've ever heard. Where does Molly come up with this stuff? Seriously.

I am going to go out on a limb and say today has been the best morning I have experienced while in Boise. I was helping Molly get dressed, and she said something about noticing that it is more difficult for her to walk in the mornings. I asked her to elaborate on the difficulty and explain what she feels and notices as different.

She told me when she first wakes up—she is a little discombobulated. That makes sense. She also said that, when she wakes up in the morning, she always craves water. So, of course I come back with, "Well, at least you don't crave walking on water in the mornings."

We both laughed, and then she said without missing a beat, "Yeah, I already do that, so I should not crave it." Oh my goodness, I laughed even harder.

I asked her, "Grams, did you just tell me you can walk on water like Jesus Christ?" She told me she would show me later, and I was somewhat trepidatious of that statement. She patted me on the shoulder, I headed to the kitchen to start our breakfast, and she headed to the bathroom.

A few minutes had passed, and I was cooking an omelet when I heard Molly say, "Jaime, come here, quick!" I obviously thought the worst, set the skillet onto an off burner, and ran into the bathroom only to find Molly laughing uncontrollably. She had dumped a bunch of water on the floor and was walking around on it. "Look, I am walking on water!"

I was half impressed with her wit and half scared she was going to slip and fall. I helped her out of the bathroom, finished making breakfast, and then cleaned up the bathroom while she was eating.

I giggled the whole morning at what Molly had done; the whole thing was just so funny. I remember when I was helping her get dressed, and she mentioned she was able to walk on water—I thought—oh that is sad—she is really starting to lose her mind—she thinks she is Jesus Christ. Ha ha, the joke was on me apparently. I have learned not to underestimate or worry about Molly.

~Minerva

January 14, 2010
Thursday

"Only God knows, and he's not going to snitch."
~Alice

This is what Molly said today when I asked her why Grandma June was holding a pumpkin in one of the pictures on the counter top. I thought I had heard it all. She also showed me this picture...

She told me about each person. She told me her daughter June was on the far left. She pointed at herself and told me that was she. She pointed out Sandy her granddaughter as the one getting married. She pointed me out last, her great- granddaughter Jaime, on the far right. Then she told me I remind her a lot of her great-granddaughter who is always making everyone laugh. I knew she was having one of those moments where she thinks I am a live-in nurse, taking care of her. She is happy, and that is all I care about.

~*James*

"It isn't the coughing you're coughing,
it's the coffin they carry you off in."
~Alice

That is just downright funny. I don't care who you are, or where you came from, when someone says something like this—you laugh—out loud.

I am not sure where Molly comes up with all these thoughts, but they are never ending. I am so glad I am writing them down, because if I attempted to recall them all later down the road, I would forget most of them. Some of these I have heard, but most of them are new to me. I love hearing these for the first time coming out of a little old lady's mouth; it just makes it that much more entertaining. Not to mention she laughs at all her own sayings, which makes it even funnier. It reminds me of Jeff Baker in junior high school.

~Minerva

January 16, 2010
Saturday

"I feel like nothing in this world
with a ring around it."

~Alice

What?

I have no idea on this one. I don't even understand what this one is attempting to convey. It is so far out there it is past my level of comprehension. How many kinds of things are in this world that have rings around them?

~ Napkins ~ ring fingers

Maybe it is literal, and it is talking about something not from this world. If that is the case, the first thing that pops into my mind is the planet, Saturn. Why would Molly feel like Saturn?

I either need a physicist or a Brit to translate this for me.

~Minerva

January 17, 2010
Sunday

"1, 2, 3, mother caught a flea, she put it in the teapot
and made a cup of tea. The flea jumped out,
mother gave a shout, Here comes the
bobby with his shirt hanging out."

~*Alice*

I am not even joking with this one. Where did she hear this? I have heard Molly sing this on several occasions. It sounds like some old nursery rhyme from England.

First, if mother did catch a flea, and it was still alive, why did she place it inside the teapot?

Second, if mother knowingly placed a flea, dead or alive into a teapot, why would she proceed to boil water in it?

Third, how did the flea jump out? Obviously, at this stage of the poem/rhyme I understand the flea has been alive this whole time. Perhaps the flea was brought back to life, but I don't really think that is the case. Did the mother take the lid off the teapot to pour the hot water into a teacup? If this is the case, how did the flea survive?

Fourth, why is the police officer coming around to this house with his shirt un-tucked? Perhaps he lives at this address, and he just finished a shift? Perhaps this particular police officer is just a sloppy dresser. Either way, showing yourself in public with your work shirt hanging out is just tacky.

~Minerva

January 19, 2010
Tuesday

"Your inner beauty exceeds your outer beauty."
~Alice

Molly says this to me at least once a day. I will do something like get her a glass of water, or make her a cup of tea, help her get into her nightgown, or help her take her dentures out and clean them, and out she pops with this phrase and a smile on her face. It's like she's a walking book of quotes. It's phenomenal and very inspiring.

Molly and I went down to the common room today, and Margaret was down there. Molly and Margaret do not get along too well. Margaret is one of those individuals who likes to one up everyone. From my best guess, I would assume it is an attempt to make her self feel better and seem more important.

Margaret asked Molly today what we were up to. Molly told her that we were going to have lunch at the Capri. Margaret immediately chimed in with, "Yeah, well, I need to go get ready because my son is coming to pick me up and we are heading to a really fancy lunch place."

I asked her where her and her son were going, and she paused for about five seconds before blurting out, "The Olive Garden." I told her that was a mighty fine, fancy place, and then I excused myself to go get my '69 Chevelle and pull it around to the front entrance so Molly didn't have to walk so far in the cold weather.

I do love the homemade food at the Capri; they really cannot be beat for the taste. The cornbread rocks, the soups rock, and the salads completely rock. One other place that I can tolerate—I'm being completely honest—is the Olive Garden. I only get their soup-salad-breadstick deal they always offer, but it rocks for the price. The minestrone soup gets a point because it is pretty tasty—especially when you dunk your breadstick in it. The salad gets two points because it has jalapenos in it.

~James

"Stop crying and get off the serpent."

~Alice

I finished working out the piano part for that song I have been working on. I am pretty excited to get it recorded at some point. I took Molly downstairs, and she listened to me play the piano for about half an hour. I love the set up of the common room. As more and more people come down to listen to me play, I can pop into the kitchen there and make them all tea or coffee. I made Molly a cup of tea before I started playing. I have found that if I bring biscuits down, she will munch on a few of them with her tea.

The bridge and chorus for the new song says:

> I give my all
> And if I should fall
> I'll get back up again and sing…
> I know my heart may break
> It's a chance I'm willing to take
> When I fall in love

69

Hold my breath and jump in
And if I can't swim
Then I need a bigger shove....

I have been keeping a close eye on Molly when it comes to our outings. She loves paying for things so I always put twenty dollars of various bills in her wallet. I want her to feel as independent and capable as possible. When we went to The Pantry this morning for tea and toast, she wanted to pay like she always does. I watched her fumble with the money today. She pulled out the ten dollar bill, the five dollar bill, and the five ones. Our total was $4.82, and she couldn't quite figure out what the money meant. I asked her if we left six dollars, did she think that would be sufficient enough to cover the total, plus a dollar and some change for the tip.

She agreed but still continued to flip through the money. I asked her if she had a five-dollar bill in her pile of wealth. She laughed and said she didn't know. So I politely pointed it out to her and said it looked like a five-dollar bill. She placed it on the table and then selected the ten-dollar bill and placed it next to the five. She placed the five ones back into her wallet and started to get up from the table. I stood up as well and felt into my back pocket, hoping I had some change on me. I did have a few ones, so as she started to walk toward the front door, I grabbed the ten and swapped it out with the one.

It is a good thing Molly does not go out by herself anymore. I can see the mishandling of money being a serious issue. Once we got home, I pulled out my little lock box and restocked Molly's wallet with the ten-dollar bill I had taken off the table, along with another five-dollar bill.

I think the main thing for me to remember is that I never want Molly to be lacking self-esteem. I want her to feel independent, and I always want her to be confident around her friends at the apartment community. I focus on the positive and not the negative. This means I focus on Molly's abilities, not her restrictions. I focus on the fact she can still walk around and eat by herself. I focus on her sense of humor and ability to partake in amazing conversations with me. I focus on her strengths—not her weaknesses.

~Minerva

Molly and I met up with June today to continue our weekly Friday ritual. The ritual starts with heading to the beauty school around nine o'clock so June and Molly can both get their shampoo–sets. After they get their hair done, we head to Denny's to grab something to eat…god help us.

Today was a special day because once every three months—Molly gets her hair re-permed. Today was the perm day, which means the students who do her hair, spend about four hours on it. So June was finished about two hours before Molly. We walked around the strip mall, meandering into the various stores. We spent a while at the dollar store, skipped the next three shops, which consisted of the floral shop, the Thai cuisine place, and the liquor store. We then made our way into Albertson's for a bit.

Grandma June and I kept going back to check on Molly every twenty minutes or so. Every time June would ask Molly how she was doing, Molly would reply with, "He who expecteth nothing is never disappointed." I could tell Grandma was getting annoyed with her hair taking so long, but I had to laugh at the situation. What else can you do?

After the good times at the Toni and Guy beauty school, I drove Molly up to the Denny's by the airport, and June followed us in her car. It always amazes me how packed Denny's is. I just don't understand how a place with food of that quality is always booming with business on the weekends. Maybe it's me. Maybe I have a strange palate; maybe I am the only one who doesn't think Denny's is quite up to par. You know, whatever. It is what it is, and ten years from now when I think back to hanging out with June and Molly, there will never be a negative thought about Denny's.

So June and Molly always get the same thing, they split the Grand Slam, which consists of two eggs, two pancakes, and two bacon strips or sausage links. I change up my order depending on what mood I'm in. Sometimes I am in the mood for breakfast, and if that is the case, I end up with the oatmeal or toast. If I am in the mood for lunch, then I get a salad—with the dressing on the side, of course.

I will say, that I do like their coffee. Perhaps it is because I water it down with so much milk and sweetener—It doesn't taste like coffee by the time I am done with it.

~*Minerva*

"Like everybody until they give you a reason not to."

~Alice

Molly and I were talking today, and we decided to make a list of things that would qualify a person as being not nice:

1. People who think they are right all the time
2. People who don't care about anyone except themselves
3. People who expect everything to be handed to them
4. People who think the world revolves around them
5. People who are jealous of others
6. People who are spoiled brats

I think this is a pretty good list. Molly talked about how people don't appreciate what is in front of them. She said kids today are so spoiled and self-centered. She told me I am a good kid who has her priorities straight, and that made me smile. I am not perfect by any means, and I may not always have my priorities straight, but I think I have a good outlook on life. I am humble and not afraid to make mistakes, which is important to me.

Molly is having an increasingly difficult time buttoning her shirts up. When I got here at the end of the year, she could button her shirt up by herself. I am now noticing she fidgets with a button until I ask her politely if I can assist her. She always smiles and agrees with me. I always keep the mentality that this is her life, and I am just here to help with anything she may need. I ask permission with anything I do, and she is always so receptive to the humility I present.

~*Minerva*

January 24, 2010
Sunday

"Put a shirt on."

~*Alice*

"Wear what you want."

~*Alice*

These are both in response to me, running around Molly's apartment in my bikini for about an hour today. I can't help it; she has the heat turned up past ninety degrees because she claims anything less is cold. Yes, Grandma Molly, if your justification is completely justified, then so is mine.

You have to love the fine line between cause and effect. Law of physics, economics—I don't care what you classify the situation as—if the heat is going to be on so Molly can be comfortable, my clothes are coming off so I can be comfortable too. I really think it's a win-win, or as Michael Scott would say, "It's a win-win-win situation."

I have to admit it's a little better when I open the windows in the living room. At least if there is some semblance of a breeze, I feel like I can breathe. So the windows stay open, and I lay on my bed—dying of heat exhaustion. Actually, I started a painting today of a bird. I am going to take it up to Mom's when I finish it. It should take me another couple hours though, as I have to wait for the paint to dry.

~*James*

"Ask no questions — and you will be told no lies."

~Alice

I have this morning ritual that I will admit to, and I will say it is in response to Molly's nightly bathroom schedule. Molly follows the same routine of waking up in the middle of the night to go to the bathroom. This happens anywhere between two o'clock and five o'clock in the morning. After the emptying of the bladder, she goes back to bed until around eight. I have been walking over to The Pantry in the mornings to enjoy a cup of coffee and read. The Pantry opens at six, Monday through Friday, so it is perfect. I can walk over there in under two minutes. I can enjoy a morning beverage, read for about an hour and a half, and then come back home before Molly wakes up.

I sit here at The Pantry—with my thoughts, my coffee, and my new and first glimpse into the literary world of John Updike. Ty from Albertson's gave me this book with a brilliant, must-read recommendation. Before about a week ago, I had never heard of John Updike. Sometimes it is so peaceful to sit in silence with myself—pondering, reflecting, and ever so slowly growing. I am practicing what I preach to myself. I am listening to the simplicity Thoreau has unmistakably wanted me to pay attention to.

Simplicity is not a hard ideal or complicated moral. It is what it is. It is what Thoreau, Emerson, and Linsley taught me. It is about appreciating the basics—not getting lost in materialism. Thank you, Boise, for the reminder of how beautiful simplicity truly is.

~Minerva

January 26, 2010
Tuesday

"I'm going out of my mind...picking blackberries."
~Alice

So, we have this new tradition...I'm not sure if that's necessarily the right word...it may be a ritual.

In the mornings, before Molly wakes up, I head to The Pantry. I drink water along with either coffee or hot chocolate, while I read and write. I met a waitress who goes by the name May. She always works the morning shift, but she doesn't seem to be a morning person. No, that is not right. She is friendly and always smiling; she just doesn't seem very awake.

Maybe it takes her a while—I don't know. I am again reading through *The Shining* by Stephen King. I remember reading that book for the first time in fourth grade. Dad brought it home for me. I remember staying up late throughout the nights—huddled under my covers—reading that book with my flashlight. The topiary scene always sticks out in my mind.

Oh my god—I just heard May ringing someone out. The Pantry uses an old-school cash register. The sound this till makes is exactly the same sound the smoke monster makes on LOST. That is too funny. I really do like that show—one season left—right?

~Minerva

January 26, 2010
Still Tuesday

"By helping other people, you help yourself."
~Alice

I'm reading this little green hardback book I have that was written by Poe, and it humbles me greatly—there's a word on almost every page that I do not know the meaning of.

turgid – congested

cessation – cease action

simcom – hot wind

deigning – condescend, stoop to action

ignes fatui – Latin for "foolish fire" - a phosphorescent light hovering above marsh grounds

pyrrhonism – skepticism

tinctured – slight mixture/tint/color of anything

antiquated – grow old, obsolete

apothegm – a short, instructive story

veracity – truthfulness, accuracy

maelstrom – whirlpool vortex

Norwegian coast, 68 degrees of latitude

I finished reading John Updike's compilation of short stories: "Trust Me." Oh, my god, "trust me" is right. Trust me to never again waste my time on reading anything John Updike has written. I really don't care you went to Harvard, and I really don't care that you are impotent. Your stories are boring, and I cannot for the life of me understand who in their right mind would publish such ordinary writings. Thank goodness for Updike my opinion counts for very little.

~*Minerva*

January 27, 2010
Wednesday

"Hope itself is hopeless."

~Minerva

Just when I think I have a decent grasp on my primary language, I go and read a book, which reminds me of how much I truly don't know. Poe's book, *Tales of Mystery and Imagination* is incredible. I am learning a large handful of new words.

Something so difficult for me seems to be so simple and of little inconvenience to certain others with immense and expansive vocabularies.

It is BINGO night, and I would be lying if I said I wasn't excited. And, no I don't want to buy one of your dobbers that you are selling for five dollars. I can purchase one down at the dollar store for a dollar plus 6 percent sales tax. And yes, I understand how important your good luck charms are to you. I fully comprehend that if you do not blow the train whistle when I-22 is called you will jinx yourself from winning that particular game. I am also fully aware that if you do not ring your little teatime bell when 0-66 is called, you have no chance of winning whatever game is being played at the time. That is made obvious every time I sit next to you.

Do you think a person like me, without any good luck charms, could be capable of yelling out BINGO four times in one evening? Because I did.

"Why is the letter crooked—and why can't you straighten it?"

~Alice

Some of these sayings are so bizarre and out there that I may never understand their true meanings, full beauty, or potential.

Today was another fun-filled day of asking Molly questions that I knew she had no clue about. The whole point is to see how creative I can get her to be.

Question 1: Topic—Harry Potter

Me: Have you seen Harry Potter roaming the halls lately?

Molly: Who?

Me: You know, that wizard guy, he is British? I saw him at the New Year's potluck; I was just wondering how he is getting on?

Molly: Oh, you know Mr. Potter; he's here, and he is there.

Me: So, he is everywhere?

Molly: Yep.

Me: He sure was hogging all the cookies at that New Year's Party. Do you think he will be at the next potluck?

Molly: I don't know, but he isn't coming anywhere near my biscuits.

Me: Maybe we should address the issue and write him a letter and tell him a thing or two about etiquette?

Molly: Someone needs to inform him of the rules around here. We aren't in Britain any more.

Me: Is it okay to hog all the cookies if you do live in Britain?

Molly: They are biscuits, and it depends on where you are from. Where did you say Mr. Potter is from?

Me: Uh, I'm not sure. Liverpool, I think.

Molly: Hmm, that would explain it.

Now that was the clue that is was time to move on to the next topic. If you dilly-dally on one certain topic for too long, Molly will figure out what you are doing.

Question 2: Topic—Swimming pool on the roof

Me: Have they finished building that deluxe swimming pool on the roof?

Molly: There's a pool on the roof?

Me: Yes, I thought it was you who told me about it. You were saying that there were going to be lounge chairs and beach balls floating in the pool. And I heard something about how they were going to serve fruity cocktail drinks with little umbrellas in them. Wasn't that you?

Molly: Probably. I don't know what is going on with the pool, but we should find out.

Molly is great. You can start in on any conversation, fact or fiction, and she just joins in. It is like she has this innate improvisational ability that is just wicked. I must have inherited my talent from her. Thanks, Molly!

~ *Nicks*

*"I'm going to think—I don't know what with,
but I'm going to think."*

~*Alice*

Molly asked me today if I thought being born again was a good idea. She says if she does decide to go that route, it might be a good idea because she would know everything she knows now, and she would want to try life as a boy. She also says if she decides to do the reincarnation thing, she is going to request that she be born again in England.

I told her I was interested in the reincarnation thing as well. I asked her whom she was going to ask permission from to be born again in England. She didn't quite know, but she was quite certain that once she passes away, someone who is in charge of the whole reincarnation process would be introduced. She seemed quite sure that she needed to talk with a reincarnation professional, because if she did not, things could go awry, and she could end up coming back as a dog or cat.

I asked her what name she would want if she were going to come back as a boy. She said either Jonathan or Alfred. She said if she comes back as a girl, she wants to be named Molly.

Mac standing next to his flat in England.

I asked her what other options she was thinking of besides the reincarnation plan. She informed me that reincarnation is "Plan A." "Plan B" is to be buried next to Mac, her second husband.

Molly said Mac is already buried up in Canada in a town called Hamilton. That is not a bad "Plan

B," if we are talking about rational outcomes I can assist her with.

I asked her if she had a "Plan C." She shook her head in disgust and informed me that if she can't have either of those options, just to put her on the curb in a trash bag. I laughed out loud. I told her that was my "Plan A," but I was having a hard time finding someone to take care of my body. She promised that if I go first, she would place me on the curb in a Hefty sack.

~Minerva

*"I don't care what you call me—as long
as you don't call me late for dinner."*

~Alice

Molly believes no child should be christened until he or she is old enough to decide for himself or herself if he or she wants to be christened or not. I was shocked when I heard this opinion of hers. Molly and I are very similar with some of our beliefs, attitudes, behaviors, and thoughts.

The fact she shared this with me is absolutely brilliant. She also said parents need to give their children three or four names—so when they get older, they can choose the name they like best.

The strangest part of the conversation was the end. Molly shared with me that she felt I could better accomplish what I was put on this earth to do if I didn't bear a child. She said she couldn't quite tell yet what it is I am supposed to do but having children of my own is not a part of the game plan.

That would explain my feelings of illness whenever I think about being pregnant and having a parasite inside of me. I am not being unkind or malicious or hateful, I am just stating the scientific facts. When babies are in the womb, they are technically parasites. A parasite is any type of organism that lives, feeds, and depends on another organism for survival. Children are fine, and, in fact, they are great for some people. I just don't want any of my own to rear and be responsible for.

Could you imagine? I still toilet paper people's houses in the summertime, biscuit cars and houses, and play truth or dare. I make announcements over the loud speakers whenever I am in a supermarket or store that has an intercom system I can figure out how to work. I am constantly doing something someone will not approve of. Am I the best candidate for being a parent? I think I will leave that up to the rest of the world. There are people out there who want to be and are happy to be parents, just like there are those of us who want and are happy to be vegetarians.

~*Nicks*

*"Qui n'a plus qu'un moment a vivre n'a
plus rien a dissimuler."*

~ *Atys, Quinault*

I am in awe right now. I think, for the first time ever, I am doing a bit of research on the name Minerva. I knew the basics: Roman goddess of wisdom, art, music, and war. I knew she was the goddess of music, but I didn't realize that mythology claims she actually invented music. How cool is that?

Now that I am educating myself a bit more–I am a little freaked out by the coincidences. Well, maybe not coincidences, but similarities that were, until today unbeknownst to me:

1. Minerva is associated with olives. I love olives. Yummy!
2. Minerva is associated with owls. I love owls.
3. Minerva's festival is March nineteenth to March twenty-third.

4. Minerva is associated with votives. I light candles all the time.

5. Minerva is the patroness of all the arts and trades, painting, poetry, medicine, and music. I am interested in all these things.

6. Minerva found men and women to be equals. She guided women with sewing, spinning, cooking, cleaning, etc. She guided men with war tactics, prudence, courage, agility, and perseverance.

If I ever get a free minute, I need to check out Jupiter and see if there is any connection. Jupiter is her father.

~Minerva

"People get angry because they are jealous."

~*Alice*

Here is my theory: String Theory.

Big Bang Theory, Drive-Reduction Theory, Quantum Theory, Cognitive-Dissonance Theory, Evolution Theory

They are all theories at the end of the day. Theorized by physicists, scientists, paleontologists, chemists, anthropologists, geologists, and philosophers. Now does that mean theoretical physicists actually exist? Or are they just, hypothetically speaking, educated guesses as well?

~*Minerva*

February 2, 2010
Tuesday

"Assume nothing. Appreciate everything."
~Minerva

This quote is my new motto. I am trying it on for the year to see how it suits me. It seems everything I already believe in—fits into this saying. Simplifying my life—one day at a time.

~Minerva

February 3, 2010
Wednesday

There is a coupon in the phonebook this week, and I really don't understand what it is attempting to portray. The coupon says:

"The same room cleaned twice!"

What does this coupon even mean? I really don't understand it—all it does is leave me with a bunch of questions.

~Why do I want the same room cleaned again?

~Didn't they clean it right the first time?

Wow, I love reading through the phone book, there are some downright gems in this thing!

~*Minerva*

"We'll find out don't you know,
so suck your finger and bite my toe."

~*Alice*

Here recently, observation has become a tool of my trade, a foundation to my hierarchy of needs if you will. The trick is to observe without assumption. Here lies a catch-22, almost an oxymoron of judgment. Predictions should be based on fact only. This is something I am practicing—and I love a good challenge.

~*Minerva*

*"I'm doing everyone and making
sure no one does me."*

~Alice

I asked Molly if she wanted to help me address valentine's cards to everyone in the building. She thought I was nuts. We drove down to the dollar store, and I picked out nine boxes with twenty-four valentines in each. They were really cute little "Hello Kitty" ones, with little heart stickers to seal each envelope with. I also took Molly by the cookie aisle and told her we should probably pick out some more biscuits to have at the apartment. She picked out some almond biscuits, some butter cookies, some chocolate chip cookies, and some custard cream biscuits.

We got back to the apartment, and I stopped by the office to talk with Lorie, the resident manager. I told her what I was doing with the valentines and she gladly fulfilled my request of the tenant list, so I know to whom I should address each card. I made tea for Molly and brought out one of each cookie. She downed them all and asked for two more. Her appetite is strong when cookies and biscuits are up for grabs.

~Minerva

"Pity she's soft—she's got nice hair."

~Alice

I bought another copy of *Les Misérables*, a version I have yet to read. I also acquired a book titled, Bulfinch's *Mythology*.

I see I am written about in the pages—I can't wait to learn more about myself.

Today I helped Molly shower again. I can't believe she can still take a shower. I have noticed it is getting more difficult for her to step into the tub. Thank goodness for all the handrails everywhere—without them, we would be taking baths. Molly still lets me help her get undressed and then climbs over the tub wall. She hangs on to the railings, and I wash her. Today, while I was washing her back, she made me laugh.

She said, "Oh, what a life. Posh people pay big bucks to have people pamper and take care of them. Not me though. I have you, and bless your heart, you help me out of the kindness of your heart."

I told her she was dang right, and I told her not to forget that little fun fact. She told me she would never forget everything I do for her. I love Molly; she is so sweet. I never would have thought in a million years that some of the kindest things to come out of her mouth were while we were showering together.

~Minerva

Superbowl XLIV

Saints versus Whomever

It doesn't really matter—I heard Saints were going, and that was it for me. I remember liking the Saints since way back in the seventh and eighth grades. I have always been a San Francisco 49ers fan, but I cheered for the Saints too, because my boyfriend at the time thought they were so great. I hope they prosper and conquer.

I have started my new mythology book—I am in love once again—and it is quite ironic and fitting, for I read of Cupid only minutes ago. I never knew he had arrows that repelled love as well as arrows that kindled love's flame and burning desire. I think there must have been a surplus at the arrow-making factory of the ones that repel love. That would explain the high divorce rate. Either that or we can blame it on the fact that Cupid is blind, and he cannot see which arrows he is pulling from his quiver. He is truly a tragic little fella with all kinds of power.

I bought some adult diapers for Molly today. This past week she has had a couple of accidents, so if I can get her to wear the adult diapers, it would be easier to change them out than the bedding. I check Molly every time she goes to the bathroom, so monitoring is not a problem. Hopefully this plan will work out. I have to address it delicately, I don't want her feeling embarrassed to any degree.

~Minerva

"Do unto others, as you wish to be done by."
~Alice

Rocky came into town today—how sweet it is. We saw Brooke, ate at Blimpies®, went and got Scotch-n-sodas from Big Bun, and hung out with Mom and Dad.

It is crazy how close we are. I miss him like mad. It's like being around the family makes it that much worse.

~Minerva

When I came to The Pantry today, there was a lady perhaps in her sixties or seventies, sitting where I normally sit. I picked one of the many other available booths and proceeded to read. I left my mythology book up at Mom's yesterday, so I opted for another one I brought with me from Portland that I have been meaning to re-read, *Animal Farm* by George Orwell.

The lady got up and headed to the register. I happened to glance where she was sitting—there was a green wallet under her booth. I went to the register and told the lady about the wallet I had seen. She smiled and thanked me profusely. I told her I would get her lovely, lime-green wallet for her, and I did.

After doing my good deed for the day, I headed back over to my newly inhabited booth and began reading Orwell's classic once again. A few minutes later, May came by to pour me some coffee. She informed me that the lady, whose wallet I had found and retrieved, had paid for my coffee.

I thought that was really nice of that lady. I know my coffee is only two dollars and a quarter, but a dollar is a dollar in my book. I appreciate that someone appreciated me. I wore a smile on my face today because respect is alive and well.

~*Minerva*

February 10, 2010
Wednesday

Rocky, Dad, Rodney, Cindy, and I went up to Idaho City today to go sledding. Oh my goodness, it was so much fun. My butt is sore—technically it's not my butt—it's my lower back. The entire area around my tattoo is black and blue. I crashed and burned a bunch of times and never had so much fun doing so. Cindy definitely wins for top wreck of the day. She nailed a tree flying down some trail Rocky convinced her to do. I knew it was a horrible idea, which is why I didn't attempt to do the trail myself.

Molly seemed very upset and angry about Rocky coming by the apartment this evening— she kept saying we were going to get kicked out. I am not sure what that was about. I asked her if she was going to be okay, and she told me no. I asked her if she wanted to talk about it after Rocky left, and she nodded her head.

Rocky and Molly.

Once Rocky left, I chatted with Molly. She wanted to know if Rocky was moving in. Once I assured her that was not the case, she felt better. I asked her if it bothered her that I was living with her. She assured me that she enjoyed having me around very much. She told me we were best friends, and she didn't want anyone intruding on our tea parties. I get what she is saying. She has become very comfortable with me: I help her eat, bathe, and dress. She trusts me.

~Minerva

February 10, 2010
Still Wednesday

"Evolution does not equal progress."

~Minerva

Here is one of my recent paintings I have been working on. It took quite a while to paint all the little sun flares. This is my tribute to "Heroes," what a fantastic show.

~*James*

February 11, 2010
Thursday

I finished up addressing the valentine cards today. Molly would shake her head every time I worked on them, but now that they are complete, it is a different story. There are 196 cards to be hand delivered throughout the entire apartment complex late Saturday evening. Molly said she wants to help deliver them. I think she is getting excited now that the hard work is done. I signed every card with both of our names, so everyone who knows her should get a kick out of receiving a valentine from us. I asked Molly what time she thought would be safe to deliver the valentines. She assured me everyone would be in bed by eight o'clock. I smiled. I told her she knows best, and we would head out to do our valentine deliveries at eight. She made sure I knew we had to have a cup of tea and some biscuits before we started the valentine deliveries.

~Minerva

February 11, 2010
Still Thursday

I have decided to make a list of the regulars who frequent The Pantry. I will give the quick run down and then explain them in detail. Here is what I have noticed so far:

Monday – Bible study group, cat lovers corner, log lady and company
Tuesday – card group
Wednesday – Washington Mutual bankers, real estate agents from across the street
Thursday – Bible study group, cat lovers corner, two guys who eat lots of jelly
Friday - Bible study group, cat lovers corner, the blonde at the fourth table from the front door, sex addiction group, mortgage trio
Saturday – banjo guys
Sunday – small church group, VFW breakfast

The bible study group meets a few times a week. The intense Bible study group consists of about a dozen middle-aged men. They discuss a wide array of topics; I cannot quite seem to catch on with the pattern for when they discuss what. Monday they discussed Jesus Christ calming the storm, and today they are discussing God's second appearance to Solomon. Who needs to attend church on the weekends when you can come to The Pantry and hear sermons three times a week?

The cat lovers also meet a couple times a week—Monday and Thursday to be exact. It is a group of three middle-aged women and two slightly younger men, who share what their cats have been up to. Today I learned Jiggles does not like crunchy cat treats. I also learned Sputnik sleeps on his back.

On Mondays I get a special treat because the woman I have labeled "The Log Lady" always comes in with a surprise guest. The Log Lady is an eccentric individual who pets her purse as if it were a cat or small dog on her lap. She does this for the majority of the time she inhabits the restaurant, and I often wonder if this behavior continues at home. To the best of my recollection, I have never seen her with the same person twice. This week she was with a woman perhaps in her early twenties who ate through about a dozen of those little Smucker's® jelly packets. Last week the woman was accompanied by a gentleman in his mid-twenties, who refused to set his cell phone down. As he ate his omelet with his right hand, his cell phone was clutched by his left hand. Thank goodness his meal did not require the use of a knife.

On Tuesdays a card group meets up at seven o'clock in the morning. Some days there are five women in the group, and some days there are six. They play bridge together sometimes. From what I have gathered, they all play in one group together, but then they also have other groups they play in separately. This week they were discussing Mildred, who is outspoken. Mildred was not there to defend herself, but I feel as if I have known her for years by the way this group was talking about her. She plays too aggressively for most of their tastes, but they agree she still plays a sharp game. One of the ladies was complaining because Mildred always seems to win high at their Wednesday group game.

Wednesday is financial day at The Pantry, the Washington Mutual group, as well as the real estate agents from across the street, come for breakfast. There are three gentlemen in each group, and they never cross paths. The real estate guys come in when the restaurant opens, and they are gone by seven. The Washington Mutual guys come in right around seven thirty. Both of these groups like to down astronomical amounts of coffee, while looking at spreadsheets and certain statistical information. The real estate guys like to discuss various clients and potential house buyers, while the bankers like to discuss goals of the week, and how those are being met.

Thursdays are repeat offenses for the Bible study group and cat lovers' corner. I call it cat lovers' corner because that group always sits in one of the huge corner booths. Thursdays are special, though, because there are two older gentlemen who come in and have a specific ritual they partake in once a week. They come in, order their coffee, and then begin eating those little Smucker's® jelly packets. The gentleman with silver hair loves orange marmalade, while his buddy with dark hair has a passion for the grape jelly. Once the desired jellies have been consumed at their table, one of them volunteers to swap out their jelly basket with another one from an unoccupied table. They then share one order of toast and strategically sift through the new basket of jellies looking for their preferred flavors.

Fridays are a cornucopia of goodness. The Bible study group and the cat lovers are back; both are joined by a wide array of other fun groups. A blonde woman comes in and sits at the fourth table from the door, along the window row. She is always by herself, and I have never heard her say anything. She always points to what she wants on the menu, and when the waitress asks if she wants coffee, the woman just nods her head and smiles. She always leaves a five-dollar tip, whether she eats a meal or just consumes a cup of coffee. She always seems to be in a pleasant mood, and she always seems to be smiling. She is a beautiful woman who is reminiscent of Marilyn Monroe—always dressed as if she is going somewhere glamorous with her gorgeous blonde locks, cut short and meticulously curled.

Friday is also host to the sex addiction group. This is the group that sits closest to me, and I have no idea why. They always sit two booths away from me, so I get to hear all the details of the daily struggle for those who just have to have sex. I don't understand what the problem is: If you want it, why don't you just have it? The group comprises three men and three women; it sounds like the beginning of a bad joke to me. They talk about daily struggles to focus on things and activities other than fornication. They talk about issues at home, work, and elsewhere.

The mortgage group comes in for breakfast on Friday. These three gentlemen are obnoxious. They talk louder than necessary, and I am pretty sure it is just for show. They discuss financial issues, obviously, but at any given moment, one of them is shooting a text to someone or checking stock exchange information.

Saturdays are when the two banjo guys come in. They never have their banjos, but that is all they seem to want to talk about. They like to compare stories. One brings up a time he played in the Chattanooga Old Timers band, and the other one retaliates with the time he played in the Boston Philharmonic. They have both been around the block several times, and I am sure each man is equally amazing.

Sundays are fairly quiet. A small church group consisting of three individuals always comes in to discuss the service for that day. They make sure the sermon is going to flow from point A to point B. A handful of individuals from the

VFW also meet up on Sunday mornings as well to have breakfast before they head off to church together. Wouldn't that be funny if they attended the church where the other three individuals went?

It is so interesting being able to identify these people with their habitual patterns. Then again, perhaps someone is saying the exact same thing about me. I am the girl who comes in to the restaurant most mornings and orders a beverage. I am the girl who is always reading something and taking notes.

~Minerva

February 12, 2010
Friday

Molly brought up the afterlife today while we were picking at our Meals on Wheels lunch, and I thought it was quite peculiar how we have the same ideas in general. She informed me today that there is no afterlife, no heaven, and no hell. You don't have to preach this story to this choir. I wanted to keep the conversation going as long as possible: It's not every day you get to have a conversation about the afterlife or lack there of with an elderly individual who thinks the afterlife promo is a bunch of malarkey.

I asked her where individuals go when they die, if they don't go to heaven or hell. She told me the individual who passes away has a meeting with an expert—someone who explains the choices of reincarnation or nothing. So I asked her to clarify the choices being reincarnation or nothing-ness. She nodded her head as a silent film star or someone from the stage would—over accentuated, making sure I got the message.

Then I asked her to explain how she became certain that someone decides if you get to be reincarnated. She didn't know the specifics, but she knew those were the options. So interesting.

~*Minerva*

February 13, 2010
Saturday

It is now eleven o'clock, and Molly and I started delivering the valentine cards at eight. She made it through the entire first floor; I am so proud of her. There are about fifty residents on each floor, so it took us about half an hour to walk from door to door and tape a valentine on each resident's door. Once we finished with the first floor, I took Molly back to our apartment, and we enjoyed a cup of tea and some biscuits. She told me delivering mail was hard work, and I told her I agreed. I asked her if she was up for delivering valentines to the second floor, and she declined. She said she was tired, so I helped her get into her nightgown and into bed. I took care of her dentures and then ventured back out to deliver the rest of the valentines.

~Minerva

February 14, 2010
Sunday

Molly and I had another amazing conversation today about humans in general. I am beginning to understand why the psychologists think some behaviors, diseases, and ideas are genetically passed down through the gene pool. Some diseases skip a generation or two. Some eye colors skip a generation or two. Some religious beliefs skip a generation or two. Grandma Molly has never been very religious—according to her. Her daughter June is not overtly religious, but I remember attending church with her quite often when I was a child. According to my mother, my father was Jesus Christ. Not literally, but in the sense of his righteousness. I remember some of it. I hear stories from others who knew him well...my dad, not Jesus.

I find myself four generations away from Molly but sharing very similar ideals. I did not grow up with this woman. I rarely saw her during the first twenty years of my life. Starting around 2000 that changed slightly. Molly, June, my brother, and I started meeting for Christmas every year at Sandy's house. Sandy is Molly's granddaughter, June's daughter, my aunt, and Jesus Christ's sister.

~Minerva

February 15, 2010
Monday

I was thinking about Grandma Molly today, and how living with her has changed my life. I know her memory is getting a bit worse from day to day, but that does not affect me negatively. I walked into this situation with my eyes and mind wide open, not knowing what to fully expect. I have come to realize I am the key to Molly's happiness. I have to adapt to her ever-changing reality, and knowing that makes life easier. I can do this quite simply with the understanding that she will progressively get worse. I know what is to come; I am beginning to face more challenges as time progresses. Sometimes Molly has a difficult time expressing what she wants to say. She does not repeat herself a bunch, but I know that is a possibility. I think I do a good job of asking her questions to keep her mind stimulated so she does not have to repeat herself. Molly is brilliant whenever we do start a conversation, she doesn't really ever lose her train of thought. She may pause from time to time, but it is only for a second or two, and I think she is looking for the

128

right words. Yesterday when we were discussing the human race, she had some incredible ideas and opinions to share. She paused two different times, and I think it was only because she was having difficulty expressing her thoughts.

~Minerva

The 2010 Bucket List – updated

- change name
- submit new words to Webster's dictionary
- submersive
- favoritest
- get book written by the deadline. This includes pictures this time
- copyright new songs
- get record printed = blue see-through vinyl - tattoos: lower – owl, cephalopod, cherry blossom upper – goddess, music, wisdom

~Minerva

I am working on a letter to Ricky Gervais. I figured since he inspires me when no one else does, I might as well share that tidbit of knowledge with him. Perhaps it will put a smile on his face to know that he inspires others, in ways he may not realize.

Ricky Gervais: First draft

Before I forget, I need to thank you. I would like you to know how grateful I am to know there are others who exist out there, who feel the same way I do about certain issues.

Specifically, you have inspired me recently in my writing—something so tainted with truth—something most find to be comical—something I understand on a deeper level than most.

You remind me it is okay to be myself—to have the beliefs I do—and to not care what anyone else thinks.

Thank you.

~Minerva

The adult diapers are working out well. Molly has no problem wearing them, because she thinks I wear them as well—and half the time I do. I do when she is getting dressed in the morning, and also at nighttime when we are putting her nightgown on. I find she is wetting them every day, usually once or twice, and on rare occasions she soils herself. I am thankful for the adult diapers although I hate the squishy sound it makes when I walk. The rule seems to be if I am doing it, Molly will do it too; if Molly is doing something, she wants me to participate as well. I can play that game, so I eat my Meals on Wheels™ and wear adult diapers...and I could care less what anyone thinks.

This evening as we took Molly's dentures out as part of our every day getting-ready-for-bed routine, she asked me if I watched over her teeth at night. I told her I most certainly did. She seemed relieved and continued on by telling me she didn't want someone coming in and taking her teeth or swapping them out. I have noticed the paranoia levels growing, and I do my best to make her feel as comfortable and as secure as possible. I told her I have a security system that I turn on every night when we go to bed, and it alarms me if anyone opens the door. She was very glad to know her teeth were safe from teeth thieves.

I am looking up the synonym of "pious." I knew it meant dedicated, but it also says:

"devoted, reverent, religious, divine, sacred."
Then for antonyms it says:

"sinful, wicked, impious, atheist."

So are they saying that atheist equals wicked and sinful? That is horrible, untrue, and straight up a lie. I am slightly offended.

~Minerva, the proud vegetarian and atheist

February 19, 2010
Friday

"America is deluded——The world is delusional."

~Jaime

Just because you won't accept the truth, doesn't mean it is not there. Just because a tree falls in the forest when no one is around——doesn't automatically mean there is no sound.

There is a law for everything: a root for all beginnings.

A path everything follows...you cannot veer from the path——it is impossible, which is a contradiction to my notion that "nothing is impossible." There is order to chaos, and I am completely okay with that. The randomness of life is not so random when you take into account the choices we make. Life is nothing but a series of choices. What time am I waking up? What am I wearing? What am I eating for breakfast? What time am I leaving for work? What route am I taking to work? Am I going to speed? Where am I going to park? Am I going to do my best? Will the boss notice I am wearing sneakers today instead

134

of pumps? Will I run down to my car on my lunch break? What am I having for lunch? Should I call Ryan and say hi? Should I work out when I get home? What am I having for dinner?

From the moment we wake up, until the time we go to bed, it is one choice after another. Choices are never-ending, and that idea in itself is quite fascinating. Every choice I make affects my life, whether I am consciously thinking about it or not. If I choose to pick up some broccoli at the grocery store, it may be that choice that leads to me bumping into my third-grade teacher at the supermarket. If I had decided on macaroni and cheese, I may have never bumped into the teacher.

~Minerva

February 20, 2010
Saturday

"All the ignorance I see is inspiration
to be something else."

~*Minerva*

"All the ignorance I see is motivation
to be something else."

~*Minerva*

Here is the new painting I finished today. My greens are limited as you can tell, but I think Max turned out identifiable, which is the goal. There is a part just under the one plant I didn't finish painting brown. I didn't notice until I had put the paints away. I will fix it next week sometime.

It is really fun; some afternoons while Grandma Molly and I are visiting I start in on one of my paintings. She does enjoy watching me paint, and she always asks what the picture is of. I told her about Maurice Sendak, the gentlemen who wrote this story, along with a few other greats of his time. This book was one of my favorites growing up. I told her about how I met Maurice in Portland at Powell's, and how he invited me to a party/gathering in Lake Oswego. I told her about how I had the amazing opportunity to spend an evening visiting with Maurice and other authors like Chuck Palahniuk, who was also at that beautiful house in Lake Oswego.

When I asked Molly what she wanted for dinner, she smiled and told me I could decide this evening—because I always let her choose. I had never really thought about that until she worded it that way.

All I am trying to do is give Molly as many choices as possible. I want her to feel independent and in control. Just because she is getting older does not mean she is not capable of making decisions. Just because her cognitive patterns are changing does not mean she has to give up her dignity. Just because she gets confused at times does not mean she has to give up making choices on her own. It is up to me to make a safe environment for Molly so she can continue making all the choices she can. It is up to me to adapt to how Molly is feeling on any given day so she can continue living a happy life for as long as possible.

Living and taking care of someone like Grandma Molly is a once-in-a-lifetime experience. I am learning so much about myself as well as Alzheimer's, which is what I think she has. I am not a neurologist or psychologist, but the symptoms and signs are there. I am not sure how the professionals handle these situations, but I will continue doing what my gut tells me. Molly is so happy, and that is all I care about.

Molly is sharing an important part of her life with me, and, in return, I am growing as an individual. I have noticed how patient I am, whether I am letting her decide what we are eating or picking out what outfit she wants to wear for the day. Molly has helped make me aware of how I speak with her. If she ever gets confused, I re-word or re-phrase what I am saying. If she ever gets frustrated, I simply re-route her. This morning is a great example of how I diffused a situation and turned her negative thoughts into positive ones.

We opened her closet door, and I asked her which outfit she would like to wear for the day. She looked confused and overwhelmed, so I presented my idea. I asked her if she would like to have a seat on the bed, while I selected a few different outfits for her to choose from. She thought that was a great idea. Molly is helping me remember that everyday is a new day, and I need to modify and simplify activities. Every day is different; some days Molly has no memory slips that I am aware of. Other days she forgets or becomes confused several different times. I am always ready to adapt to her moods, behaviors, and reality.

~James

February 21, 2010
Sunday

I have come to notice that Molly seems to work best with structure. Not that I am being strict by any means, but by presenting and sticking with a routine, she seems more confident and sure of herself. We get up in the morning, and she uses the restroom. We select an outfit for the day and then eat. Sometimes we head into the living room/dining room area to have some tea, eat breakfast, and check on the world. Other times Molly feels like going out for breakfast, so I jump on the opportunity to get her out of the building. We make sure to consume plenty of tea and biscuits throughout the day. Molly and I eat lunch when the Meals on Wheels™ people deliver her meal, and we eat dinner in the evenings before having more tea and biscuits.

Molly does love tea and biscuits. It seems we consume tea and biscuits after every activity. We get dressed in the morning and then have tea and biscuits. Check the mail and then have tea and biscuits. Listen to me play the piano and then have tea and biscuits. Eat lunch and then have tea and biscuits. Walk down the hall and then come back to the apartment for tea and biscuits. Get our nightgowns on and then have some tea and biscuits. It's a good thing I love Molly so much. I have never consumed so many damn cookies in my life. She doesn't want to eat though, if I am not eating—so it is a catch-22. To be honest, I wouldn't trade this experience for anything in the world.

~Minerva

February 22, 2010
Monday

Mandarin Mondays, only here in Boise, Idaho.

I met Grandma June at the Mandarin Palace today, and they were all complaining about a mutual friend of theirs who had just passed away. It was so great; they were upset because the funeral had been set for today. The bridge players thought it was rude to schedule a funeral on a well-known, weekly recurring bridge day. So priceless. These women actually skipped the funeral of a friend because it was scheduled on the day they get together and have lunch and play bridge. Well, I am sure they have all been to their fair share of funerals to begin with, so maybe they are just becoming more inconvenient at this point.

Molly and I went to Wal-Mart to pick up her new bedding. The "High School Musical" sheet set I showed her was primarily gold, which is a color she really likes. She agreed the sheets were pretty, and I don't see the harm in purchasing a "High School Musical" bedsheet set for my great-grandmother if she likes it. How many other great-grandchildren or even grandchildren can say their great-grandmother or grandmother was cool enough to have a "High School Musical" sheet set?

Molly does have an issue with money, though. She is just like my grandfather was. If it costs more than two dollars, she is not interested. Well, the breaking point is not always two dollars, but the point is this: If it is not a good deal, she doesn't want it.

I told her the bed sheets were originally sixty dollars, and she about had a heart attack. I told her that was the original price. Then I told her they got marked down 50 percent because the gold color is not popular and not selling as well as they thought it would. That puts our total down to thirty dollars. Then I told her there was an After-Valentine's-Day sale still going on for a few more days, which marks the bed sheet set down to ten dollars.

She was starting to look more impressed, and I was running out of imaginary discount ideas. I told her we get an additional 50 percent off on Mondays with my Wal-Mart member card, so that put our sheet set at five dollars. She was happy with that explanation. If Molly would have seen the receipt, which shows that I paid almost forty dollars for that bedroom set, she probably wouldn't be walking this earth.

We got back to the apartment and put the new sheet set on Molly's bed. She was so happy to have new sheets. I asked how long it had been since she had new sheets, and she informed me she has never had new sheets. I asked her where she got the sheets that were previously on her bed. She thought about it and then informed me they were probably here when she moved in. Sometimes it is really hard for me not to laugh at the things Molly says. Not because I want to laugh at her, but the things she says are so brilliant and remind me of something I would hear an improv artist say.

~Minerva

Before me lie so many options: I am having a hard time picking one. It comes down to what I know versus what I don't. Too many options are better than not enough though. There is truth in the saying, "It could always be worse."

My mind is always going, always thinking, always pondering. Seeking answers, craving truth, separating it from the hoards of bullshit that seems to grow on trees. Hmmm, that is an interesting mixed metaphor. Money is bullshit. So maybe, metaphorically speaking, money does grow on trees.

I was working on a painting today and chatting with Molly. I asked her if she liked to paint, or if she had ever painted while growing up. She told me painting was not really her thing. She told me that she enjoys instruments though. Although she did not play any musical instruments growing up, she likes listening to music. She said she really enjoys listening to me play the piano downstairs.

We also talked about her grandson David, who happens to be my father. She remembers him being in a band, and she remembers going to watch him perform from time to time. She did not like that he was always playing in bars, but nonetheless, she did go see him play a few times. I never knew that until today, which is pretty cool. I like learning about my family history, especially anything pertaining to the musical side of things.

I finished up the section of the painting I was working on and then asked Molly if she would like to go downstairs and listen to me play the piano for a while. She said that would be a great way to spend our afternoon. I grabbed a bunch of biscuits, and we headed down to the common room. I helped Molly get comfortable on the couch, made her a cup of tea, and set the tin of biscuits next to her so she could munch away at her leisure.

~Minerva

RICKY GERVAIS: SECOND DRAFT

Because humanity does not surprise me anymore and because I have found that the secret to being happy relies on me, I am not relying on or expecting anything from anyone.

I am not truly expecting this letter to actually ever reach you. I know it would have to clear a myriad of hoops. I do, however, entertain the idea that this letter might somehow weave its way through the tapestry of bullshit agents, political propaganda hoops, and unnecessary screenings to actually wind up in the hands of the intended recipient.

I stumble across experiences that inspire me, not only as a writer, but as a person. I have come to realize that you have inspired some of my best work. I am not going to assume I know anything about you specifically. I do, however, feel I know you somewhat through your writing.

The truth of the matter is that I am quite the misanthrope. People assume that I am miserable because I have a strong dislike for the ignorance

147

of humanity. Perhaps people assume that because I am the contentious cynic I am unhappy with life. Nothing is further from the truth.

I appreciate every day—knowing I don't know when it will be my last. I love unconditionally, and I do what I want—when I want. I do it all for me, because I don't have ulterior motives to make the "A group" of after-lifers. I am thankful I can admit to myself that I don't know a lot, in retrospect, and I am damn thankful I am able to point out ridiculous beliefs and preposterous assumptions when I see them.

If I ever pass you in the streets or perhaps we cross paths at an airport or hotel, I may give you a big smile in return for your undeniable inspiration.

~*Minerva*

February 26, 2010
Thursday

I need to move my bed away from the wall. I am tired of having dreams about Roseanne and Dan Conner. Jerry lives next door and the poor man is hard of hearing. His television is turned up way too loud. His television must be right on the other side of this wall. I know exactly when "Roseanne" comes on because I wake up at some point during the episode. Last night I was dreaming about basketball. I was playing basketball at school, and then Dan Conner showed up on the court. A few nights ago I had a dream about boating and D.J. was out in the water. I blame Jerry next door. I cannot handle my dreams being invaded by the Conners for much longer.

~*James*

March 1, 2010
Monday

I woke up about one in the morning to Molly saying, "Hello...Hello...are you here?"

I went to her room and found her and her bed covered in feces. She asked what happened, and I suggested to her that maybe she pooped her pants. She was shaking her head; that definitely was not what she wanted to hear. She informed me someone had made a mess in her bed. I agreed with her completely and asked her if she wanted me to help her get cleaned up.

We got her up, and I walked with her across the hallway and into the bathroom to begin the clean up process of her body. When I turned on the bathroom light I was welcomed by a myriad of shit footprints on the floor. The shit footprints accompanied shit handprints and fingerprints everywhere on the counter, walls, toilet, towels, pictures, mirror, and candles. Surprisingly, there were none on the toilet paper. The whole ordeal really stunk, no pun intended, and added to my memorable morning.

I got Molly in the shower and hosed her down. While she was playing in the water, I scrubbed down the bathroom floor real well with the help of Mr. Clean, who I am sure is a member of the Aryan Nation. I shut off the shower water and gave Molly her big towel to wrap up in, while I grabbed another big towel to put down on the floor for her to stand on. I scrubbed the toilet and had Molly sit on the toilet lid, wrapped up in her big, furry towel, while I ran into her room to clean it. I took all the bedding off and replaced it with new clean sheets. I was so speedy and quick—I bet it was two minutes tops.

After that I carried Molly into the bedroom so she wouldn't step on the carpet. I couldn't rent a carpet cleaner until morning, and I didn't want her feet getting dirty again. I got Molly settled in bed and laid down a couple of towels on the floor in case she got up again during the early morning. I went back into the bathroom and scrubbed the walls and the counters, and damn right, I opened the living room windows—both of them.

After the scrub down, I took a shower and got ready for bed. I walked into the kitchen to grab one of my bottled waters—only to find shit footprints trekked throughout. I forgot my water and went to grab the cleaning supplies out of the hall closet. I scrubbed down the kitchen floor, the counters, fridge, and the walls of the kitchen until I was completely satisfied there was no more feces anywhere...I thought about "Vapoorize"—that stupid product Jack Black invented in the movie, *Envy*.

I took another shower, grabbed an oversized shirt to sleep in, finally lay down, and looked at the clock—just after four in the morning—nice! I slept for about three hours before my internal clock decided it was time for me to wake up.

~*Minerva*

March 2, 2010
Tuesday

I helped Mom and Dad install the new door handle on the front door—that was fun. Poor Dad was hobbling about with his Idaho City knee injury. I headed to Grandma's about six thirty and made French toast for our dinner. She loved it. We ate and watched *BrideWars*; I think she liked that as well.

Here is a highlight of the day: While I was at Mom's house I went through one of the boxes in my old bedroom. It included these items: an autographed vinyl record of Bighorn—whoever the hell that is, all of Dad's yearbooks, and a board game I made for a school assignment back in 1993 titled, "Jews and Nazis." The teacher gave me a 95 percent and commented, "What a great idea for a game." I am a little scared because the object of the game is to successfully hide if you are a Jew and to find the hidden Jews if you are a Nazi. Why would any teacher in their right mind validate or approve a game like that? I know I was just being a smart ass when I created it. Oh well,

I can't give a teacher a hard time for promoting creativity.

I was thinking about Molly this evening. I can tell she is getting more confused as the days go on. I do not know if she understands, and then, in turn, denies that she is getting closer to her time because she is scared—or if the disorientation in her brain is legitimate. Either way, I know helping ease and take away her confusion seems to keep her happy.

The forgetting who I am seems to come in waves. Nothing seems to be a permanent loss, only temporary, which is strange. When I first got here a few months ago, Molly could go days knowing I was her great-granddaughter. Then it became once or twice a week she would go through a pattern of thinking I was a live-in nurse for fifteen minutes, half an hour, or an hour. Now we are at the point where once or twice a day she thinks I am a live-in nurse. As far as Molly's comfort levels are concerned, who I am is not an issue at all because Molly likes both her great-granddaughter and the live-in nurse.

~Minerva

I am enjoying my way through Bulfinch's *Mythology*——it is one of my favorites. It has taken me a little longer than my normal completion times, but every book is different. This book deserves a lot of my time, and I am enjoying taking heavy notes within its pages. Which is reason number one why I do not like to check books out from the library. Don't get me wrong, the library is great for 90 percent of the books out there I want to just read. The other 10 percent though——I want for myself. I want to mark in them and learn them inside and out. I want that other 10 percent at my disposal any time I get a craving. I cannot, nor will I ever, get enough——I always crave more.

Molly seems to be different from most other elderly individuals. She never really gets bitter and angry. There sometimes confusion as in when I reminded her today that Friday was almost here, and we would be going to the Toni & Guy School to get her hair done. She asked if we were going this coming Friday, and I told her we were. I also reminded her that we were going to Denny's afterward with June.

Molly perked up after that comment because she likes Denny's. I am happy she still likes to go out because, when we first got the walker, Molly was not a happy camper. It was an independence issue at that point, and she did not want help from anyone or anything, including that walker.

These past couple months have been monumental in the respect of Molly's progress with admitting defeat when it comes to certain freedoms. The walker is perhaps one of the biggest. She has no problem now going out in public with her walker. I don't know if she realized that if she wants to go out, she has to use it, or if she has subconsciously blocked that hatred for having to give up a bit of independence in her brain.

Denial is a very powerful tool.

I have read many psychology books that explain how denial can lead to repression, and that is how the brain protects itself from certain traumatic experiences. Perhaps there is not much difference mentally between a child who is physically abused and an elderly individual whose Alzheimer's symptoms are progressing. The child has the ability to deny and repress sexual assaults, which in turn protect the child from having to remember the awful experience(s). Perhaps the elderly have a similar ability to deny and repress hardships such as having to give up certain independence like walking without assistance, showering without assistance, or living in general without assistance. Perhaps the denial and repression allow the elderly individual to live a happier, child-like life, without care or worry.

~Minerva

2005. Molly and I walking along the boardwalk in Seaside, Oregon.

March 4, 2010
Thursday

~Trust my cause to the strife of deeds.

~Like the sea, which receives all the rivers, yet is never filled up.

~This is the best insult for anyone who demands too much, for anyone who takes and takes.

~So blind is the lust of gain.

~People are not always what they pretend to be.

~Carpenters the music group, not the Jesus fan club.

Molly was in using the restroom this morning and when she came out she was slightly irritated. She informed me Mr. Potter had been in her bathroom again using her toilet paper. I was shocked she even remembered that I brought up Harry Potter. I now know to never doubt the severity and importance of a woman's bathroom. I told her I would tell Mr. Potter that he wasn't welcome anymore in her apartment.

She went to the hall closet and opened it. I asked her if I could assist her with anything, and she had me get out a shoebox filled with blank cards. Cards for every occasion filled this antique shoebox; Christmas cards, birthday cards, thank you cards, Easter cards, Good Friday cards, Martin Luther King Jr. cards, Queen's birthday cards, Memorial Day cards, Halloween cards, Boxing Day cards, Thanksgiving cards, "get well soon" cards, and I'm sure a few blank ones as well.

Molly scanned through them and pulled out a cute, masculine type card with mallard ducks in a pond on the front of it. It was blank on the inside. She asked me to hand her a pen, which I did. She began a short message addressed to Mr. Potter. When she was finished, the note said, "Mr. Potter, it has come to my attention that you are using my toilet paper. Please stop this nonsense immediately. Thank you, Alice McWhirter, 4208."

It was everything I could do to keep a deadpan face. She closed up the card and placed it in the little envelope made just for that card. She addressed it to Mr. Potter and told me we needed to take the card over to his apartment immediately. I told her I would do it after we ate breakfast. She was ready to go though; she wanted Mr. Potter to get the message as soon as possible. I told her I would walk the note over and then come back to make breakfast. That still wasn't good enough. She wanted to hand deliver the message to Mr. Potter himself. I had no idea how this was going to turn out. I told her to have a seat because we needed to put her shoes, as well as my shoes, on.

Putting on shoes bought me enough time to figure out what to do. Molly wanted to give the card to someone, so I figured I would take her to Joe's apartment. Joe is a guy who appears to be about thirty years of age, who lives down on the second floor. Joe is a little slower than average, but he is one of the nicest guys I have ever met. I met him at the New Year's party, and he invited me up to his apartment sometime to show me some of his artwork. So Molly and I walked down to the elevators and rode then to the second floor. I prepped her on the way down, I told her to be polite and just give him the card. I told her there is no sense in being mean to his face because we are better than that; she agreed, thank goodness.

We got to Joe's apartment, and I knocked on the door. Joe opened the door and smiled. If only I had been able to prep him with the Harry Potter backstory. Joe wished us a good morning, and Molly handed him the card. Molly told him the card was for him and then informed Joe we were off to eat breakfast.

Joe looked slightly confused; I am sure he was wondering why we brought him a card. He thanked us for the card, and Molly started walking off. I quickly whispered into his ear that the card was not for him and to please hang on to it for me—I would be back down later to get it from him. He nodded his head and closed the door. I caught up with Molly a few doors down, and we finished walking to the elevators together.

I know what this means. This now means I have to keep a close eye on Molly's toilet paper. If her little counter stash ever runs out, she will think Harry Potter has been in her apartment after she specifically told him to stop. I cannot allow that to happen, so now I am officially on toilet paper duty. I really don't see it being a problem; I am in the bathroom, cleaning up after Molly, every time she goes in there. Did she wipe properly? Check. Did she wash her hands? Check. Is there toilet paper squares on the counter? Check.

I went back down to Joe's apartment around noon. Here is how that conversation went:

Me: Hi, Joe.

Joe: Hi, Jaime. Why did Molly confuse me with Mr. Potter?

Me: Well, Molly's memory is not as good as it used to be, and I told her that you were Harry Potter. I shouldn't have, but I did.

Joe: Harry Potter? I am not Harry Potter!

Me: I know you are not Joe; you are cooler than Harry Potter.

Joe: You really think I am cooler than Harry Potter?

Me: Absolutely. Harry Potter can't draw like you can.

Joe was smiling by the end of the conversation. He gave me the card back and agreed the Harry Potter ordeal was something we could share just between the two of us. He is such a nice man, and I am really happy with how that whole ordeal went down. I can only imagine what would have happened if Molly would have wanted to be confrontational about the toilet paper issue. Thankfully, most individuals are not confrontational types.

Molly and I had a wonderful afternoon talking about when she worked for a store called Betty Feeney's Decorator Shop. It was a little store with tons of eclectic items owned by Betty Feeney Griffin. She owned her main store downtown, and then had several other little annex stores as well as the Lampshade Shop. Molly said she passed away in January of 2003; apparently, she was in her late seventies. I remember going to the mall with my best friend Carol, when we were in elementary school. One of the Betty Feeney Annexes was in the mall, and Carol and I would go see if my great- grandmother was working. If she were, I would say hi and give her a hug. Nothing beats good times and wonderful memories.

~James

I came home from The Pantry this morning about seven thirty, and Molly was asleep in my bed. I woke her up and asked her if she wanted to go get into her own bed. She said she didn't know whose apartment she was in, and she was extremely confused. I got her up out of the bed, and she wanted to go to the bathroom.

Afterward, she stood in the hallway and asked where she was supposed to go. I showed her to her room and asked her if it looked familiar. I walk in first, and she followed me. I sit on the bed with her, and she asks me if I will explain what is happening. She claims it isn't her room, and she is looking very sad at this point. So I jump in and tell her we have moved apartments, but I tried to decorate it like her old place.

We ate breakfast, and I told her we needed to switch apartments because there was a fire in the old building. She was completely fine after that. She said it was starting to feel like home, and I did a fantastic job decorating it to look like her old place. Yay, two points for diffusing the situation and helping Molly feel better. She is doing a fantastic job of keeping me on my toes.

~James

I found this picture of Rocky in my dictionary. That is so funny and such a cute picture. I can tell it was taken at Grandma June's.

~ *Nicks*

March 10, 2010
Wednesday

I received a flier in the mail today for Washington Mutual. They are attempting to gain some more customers by bribing individuals like myself with free gifts. Washington Mutual has gone above and beyond what I would expect of any bank; they are giving out a free, twenty-four-piece Tupperware set.

Here is my question, if I open a checking account with the Washington Mutual people, do I just get the free Tupperware, or does the Tupperware come with all the goodies I see here in this picture as well? The picture is so beautifully arranged: the bigger pieces in the back, smaller ones in the front. It truly is a stair-step design masterpiece.

I didn't find a disclaimer in the small print anywhere stating the status of the Tupperware interior. It looks like I might be the lucky recipient of some Froot Loops® and bubble gum.

The thing is, if I actually thought there was the slightest chance to receive any of the goodies shown here for free, I would already be down at the bank. And what are those items in back stacked on the far left? Are those lime rinds underneath the smaller container of Froot Loops®? I don't want any lime rinds!

~Nicks

March 11, 2010
Thursday

So at this point Molly seems to be doing well, although I can tell her Alzheimer's is progressing. I am sure every individual is affected in slightly different ways and at slightly different paces. When I moved in with Molly, she needed help showering and that was the biggest issue I saw. When I initially moved in, I also noticed she didn't want to eat, but I solved that problem by offering to eat together.

The primary changes include these: She needs assistance with getting dressed, prepping all meals, and putting her shoes on. I can tell her memory is fading a bit more.

She still remembers the names of everyone who occupies the building, which is quite impressive. She does not technically remember everyone in the building. I meant she still remembers the names of all her friends and acquaintances that occupy the building. If I had to make an educated guess on how many people she is a friend with in the building, I would say around a hundred individuals.

Molly still finds her mailbox without help. She always makes her way back to her apartment as well, which I thought might become a problem at some point. She has lived in two different apartments here in the complex during the past forty years, and I thought confusion might lead her to the old apartment at some point.

Molly still picks out which outfits she wants to wear for the day, and she still gets around with her walker. She is a bit slower now compared to a few months ago, but she always tries her best. That is all that matters. She has a wonderful outlook on life and never really seems to be angry or bitter. She is pleasant to be around and is always cracking jokes and trying to make me smile. She succeeds brilliantly, never having to try very hard.

As the days pass, I realize certain tasks become harder and sometimes impossible for Molly to complete by herself. I focus on her strengths and remember we all have weaknesses.

I have decided that the money thing is getting out of hand. This morning we went to The Pantry for breakfast, and I tried a new tactic to see if it would work. I told her I was going to pay for breakfast because she always pays. She said that is what good grandmothers do. I smiled and retaliated with the compromise that I pay this time, and she pays next time. It worked, and she let me pay.

I will try this tactic again when we go to the store later today. If it does work, I can leave a few ones in her wallet so if she checks, there is some money there. I am always with her though, so there should never be an issue with her giving someone too much or too little money. I should be able to diffuse the confusion she finds with currency by using the excuse that it is my turn to pay.

~Minerva

March 13, 2010
Saturday

I need to write out my pieces for the comedy routines. I have maybe twenty to thirty minutes of material—if told right. Make sure to cover the tollbooth barter and the Dealey Plaza Shooting Range.

The tollbooth barter bit is this: Start out with a simple story that gets progressively more outrageous. The scenario is that you either didn't realize you were running into a tollbooth, or you do not have change. Either way, you are unprepared. What if there was a lane for barters?

You could offer up something of equal or greater value? For example, "I'll give you this unopened pack of Dentine Spearmint flavored gum valued at seventy-nine cents and this cool keychain I picked up at the local credit union."

Then, the toll booth-barter-operator on shift could either accept or decline the offer. It would be great. Other trades could include; Hannah Montana CDs, a Bible—KJV, iPod, shoes. Start swapping; I will give you my iPod—8 GB, for the Cyndi Lauper vinyl and the stuffed Easter bunny.

The Dealey Plaza shooting range in Boise, Idaho, would be a great replica location of the site of President Kennedy's assassination. You get to choose where to stand: The options include the grassy knoll, the book depository, and other random spots. Then the replica car comes around on an automated track, and you get to shoot at the replica president and replica John Connally. The goal is to repeat the incident from December of 1963. Can you, with a single bullet, have it pass through the president and the governor's chest, wrist, and thigh?

Provide karaoke at the DMV: Is there a better way to spend your time waiting for your number to be called at the DMV? You walk in, you take a number, and you pick a song. Oh, look, I am number sixty-three, and I think I am in the mood to sing something by The Cars. The boards that light up in the front of the room could have numbers on one board and songs on the other, that way, people who were up next to sing their song could get prepared.

Heavy metal song—first attempt of "Get Outta My Way."

Chorus: So get out of my way, you are in my lane, you have no place go back inside, you have no clue, what you should do, so I'm telling you get outta my way.

Verse: Sometimes I want to go for a drive, but once I get behind the wheel, everyone is self-absorbed so I—can't decide how I should feel.

Bridge: Let it build, let it fester, and grow—aggression, repossession.

I am quite proud of myself. Living with Molly is a constant and ever-changing complexity of problem-solving challenges. She wants her independence, and that is completely understandable. The issue with her wanting to pay all the time seems to be diverted for the time being with my tactic of telling her it is my turn to pay because she paid last time. She seems to see the logic within that argument and is allowing me to pay for things for the time being. One day at a time though, I don't want to get too comfortable with an idea because that will be the time she throws a curve ball my direction.

~Minerva

Molly seems to be getting tired of the Meals on Wheels™ menu, so I started eating half of them with her. They aren't bad. I just have to pretend I am eating the meat or make sure she has all the meat on her plate to begin with. Today worked out great. She ate the half of her Meals on Wheels™ food at lunch, and then I told her I would start cooking us whatever she thinks sounds good for dinner. She really liked the idea of me sharing her Meals on Wheels™ meal for lunch and then having me cook dinner for us. This evening she wanted spaghetti with meatballs and parmesan cheese. I have a fantastic little recipe for meatballs from the time when I used to eat meat. I just winged it on the amounts and made her a dozen little meatballs about the size you would find in a can of Chef Boyardee®. She ate six of them, that little cow! She tried one with teriyaki sauce, and she said it was absolutely delicious. She ate the spaghetti and then ate the meatballs separately with the teriyaki sauce smothering the meat. As long as she wants to eat and enjoys eating, I am a happy camper.

~James

Molly woke up this morning and asked me when we were going back to her place. Of course, I needed to make sure we were on the same page, so I asked her to kindly remind me where we were. She replied, "Your place. I remember going for the drive yesterday, which was very lovely, dear. Then you brought me here to your place. It is very nice, but when are we going home?" I told her we would head home shortly after breakfast.

My thinking was perhaps by the time breakfast was over, she would realize we were in her apartment without me having to take any action on this misperception. We got dressed and headed out in the living room to have breakfast. She sat down at the table, and I headed into the kitchen to make some pancakes.

She started looking around and noticing things, "Hey," she said and was so excited that I was glad I was there to share in the excitement.

"I have a couch just like that one, in my place!" She was pointing to her own davenport.

"Yes, you do, Grandma," I replied with a smile on my face. I figured she would get it eventually, that all the stuff was hers to begin with. She legitimately didn't know.

"And I have pictures just like these two in my apartment. I think they are in the exact same spot!" She seemed absolutely amazed that we somehow magically and irrationally happened to have the exact same taste with our apartment set-ups.

"Wow, Grandma," I was totally being facetious at that point—I have to play along. Those are my two options. Go along with what she believes and keep her life simple, or, correct and confuse her. The choice seems blatantly obvious to me. "That's pretty amazing—we have the same taste," I chimed in.

"Yeah," She was totally smiling at this point. "I have the same picture of us as well." She was pointing to the picture that was taken at Sandy's wedding. The idea of being at my place continued on through breakfast. We took a walk around the complex and then came back upstairs because Molly wanted to take a nap. When she woke up, it was as if nothing had shorted out earlier in her brain. She knew exactly where she was, and who I was.

March 17, 2010
Brooke's birthday
Wednesday

Molly woke up this morning and asked where everyone had wandered off. I had no idea what she was thinking or where she thought she was, so I again asked some questions to help me figure out the puzzle of where we supposedly were. I asked, "Who are you talking about Grandma? Who has disappeared? I see you and I are still here, so that is good."

She started in immediately with, "Sandy and June and Rocky—where are they? Are they even here yet?" This is one of those moments I try and rack my brain—let it fill with assumptions—trying desperately to get on the same page as grandma.

Being with Molly is a challenge, and it is the biggest brainteaser I have ever faced. Do not get me wrong; it is a blast and a new adventure every day. I'm stoked and excited because with dementia and Alzheimer's, every day is spontaneous fun if you ask me. "I don't know, Grandma, they are here somewhere. I am just not sure what they are doing." I kept my answers vague.

Molly chimed right back to me with the helpful clue, "Well, is Sandy still down at the pool?"

That question was a big help for me, and I was starting to think Molly believed the family was at the Oregon coast. There were about half a dozen times when our small family would get together and spend time around each other. The Oregon coast seemed to be a popular destination point for the family.

"Yes, she is," I replied, "She should be back up here soon."

"Well, when are we leaving?" She always asks that question when we are somewhere besides her apartment. Whether reality confirmed or denied our existence in her apartment was beside the point. The only reality that matters is Molly's.

"Tomorrow morning, is that okay?" I'm giggling to myself at this point.

"Oh, yeah, this place is great, I like it here. Are the people still downstairs dancing?" Now she is confusing me, because I do not remember ever being anywhere where there was dancing taking place. At least she liked wherever she thought we were staying with the family.

"No, Grandma," I replied, "No one is dancing downstairs at the moment."

"Oh well, that was fun to take a walk down there last night and see them."

She has a huge smile on her face. It is one of those faces that look like she is messing with me. It is almost as if she knows I will not call her out on her shenanigans.

"Where's June? Is she still looking for sand dollars?"

"Oh yeah, most definitely. Her and Rocky are both down on the beach looking for sand dollars." I'm having fun at this point. "They said they weren't coming back until they found seven dollars and fifty cents worth."

"Oh well, should we go downstairs at lunchtime to see what they are going to feed us?" She keeps asking about downstairs, and I am assuming she thinks that wherever we are staying has some sort of buffet-style lunch.

"Um, yeah, maybe that's a good idea." I finished making Molly breakfast. We talked about Oregon for a while, and then I told her I needed to run to the grocery store. I asked her if she wanted to go, and she politely declined. I went by myself, grabbed some orange juice and bananas, and came back to the apartment. Molly had her jacket and shoes on, and she was heading for the front door. "Where are you going, Grandma?"

"Downstairs, dear, I thought you said we were leaving," She looked at me with hopeful eyes.

"Yes, should we get out of here and go get something to eat? I'm starving." I was hoping she would go along with my game plan and agree with me.

"Yeah, where are we going?" She looked excited.

"Well, not far. Somewhere really tasty and really special though." I was planning on taking her to The Pantry. We got downstairs and in the car to drive over to the restaurant. By the time we had walked inside and got seated, she had forgotten all about the Oregon coast, and she knew we were in Boise. We had some pancakes and coffee and enjoyed the rest of our day in this reality.

~James

March 18, 2010
Thursday

I wake up with Molly hollering—well, she doesn't really holler—she just says, "Hello? Hello?" Her hellos are about ten seconds apart—each one more hopeful than the last. I get up; it's about five o'clock in the morning, and I head to her bedroom. The nightlight in the bathroom is the only light in the entire apartment that gives me visibility. Molly's bed is vacant and her walker is right next to the bed, which is where she leaves it when she goes to sleep every night. I turn around and don't see her when I look across the hallway into the bathroom.

"Grandma, where are you?" I am waiting for her response.

"I'm over here!" She is excited I have come to her rescue. I follow her voice around to the far side of the bed. I have found Molly, she is between the bed and her long dresser; she is lying on the floor and has wedged herself underneath her big poofy chair.

"Can you get me out? They put me here!"

"Who put you under the chair, Grandma?" I can't wait to hear her answer; I'm trying not to smile.

"The people. They know that I know." She sounds very convincing at this point.

"What do you know, Grandma?" I started moving her from under the chair. Well, technically, I had her move her hands because she was hanging on to the legs of the chair. After I got her hands down by her side, I lifted the chair up and away from her. I moved it over to the other side of the room and then came back over to pick up Grandma.

"I don't remember, but they know that I know, that's why they did this." Her reasoning made absolutely no sense to me whatsoever. I helped her sit up and lean against the bed at this point.

"Well, what should we do about this, Grandma?" Here comes the part when some individuals will say that I'm not really helping the situation, but the lines are gray, so who really knows? I know I would never in a million years do anything intentionally to make her existence worse than it already is.

"Grandma, should we call the police?"

"No, we cannot do that. We need to look for clues. They must have left something behind. Help me up so we can look."

At this point, there is no stopping Molly, she is motivated and ready to hunt for clues. I lift her up onto the bed, and she takes it from there. She gets up off the bed to begin looking for clues.

"They came in and knew that I knew." She is looking around her room for only God knows what. I am trying to not laugh out loud, while keeping my stone poker face on to help her look for—I don't even know what. It reminded me of Harry, Ron, and Hermione looking for Voldemort's Horcruxes. I got Nagini, the ring, the diary, and the locket so far…who knows what other objects I need to find at this point?

"They didn't say anything, they just put me where it would be hard to get to me. They are trying to scare us. We aren't going to be scared, though, are we? This is our place, and we are not putting up with this!"

I am a permanent, alternative reality, dementia cheerleader. I continue fueling the fire, agreeing with her, making her feel loved, and enjoying every minute of it.

"No, we are not putting up with this," I chime in to let her know I am supporting her decision. "We are not going to be scared!" I continue pretending to look for clues.

"Oh we've hit the jackpot—oh, here it is!" I have never heard Molly sound so excited in my entire life. She bends down and picks up one of her used Kleenex tissues.

"They left this behind, and they didn't think we would notice!"

"Sweet!" I am dying at this point. I want to laugh out loud so hard. I can tell it is a tissue, but I have no idea what she thinks it is.

"What is it, Grandma?"

"It's a note!" She starts unfolding her used tissue until it is completely unfolded. "I can't read what it says—can you?" She handed me the Kleenex. I had to make something up, the excitement and tension of not knowing was totally getting to her.

"It has your name and your address, Grandma." I looked at her with intensity.

"I knew it!" She snatched the tissue out of my hand. "I knew that they knew I knew!"

I giggled out loud at this point. Maybe it was a snicker, I can't really remember. That was a line-for-line, word-for-word reminder of the Peter Gabriel song I used to sing to my brother.

"Grandma, what are we going to do? Is this getting out of hand?" I am wondering what she is going to suggest.

"We need to lock the doors at night and be sure to listen for them. They may come back." She looks at me to make sure I'm paying attention.

"Yes, I think that is a great plan. We also need to pretend that we don't know anything, and that will really throw them off!" I just waited for her to respond.

"Yes, but don't forget that I know." It's like she needs to make sure we are on the same page.

"I know, Grandma. You and I both know that they know. We know, but we won't let them know that we know!" I'm dying so hard at this point on the inside. I wish I could have recorded the entire conversation. "Let's get you dressed and have some breakfast." We got up, had some pancakes and eggs for breakfast, and Molly did not mention the incident again—or the fact that they knew she knew.

~*James*

Happy birthday, little broseph. That sounds funny. I'm so excited to see him on Monday.

Molly and I had a wonderful talk about her and Mac, her second husband.

1954 Molly and Mac at home in Canada.

1961 Molly and Mac fishing Lake Ontario, California.

Molly talked with me a little about World War II and some of what she remembered. According to Molly, her first husband, who was June's father, was injured in the shipyards during the war. His name was Mason Gladwin, and he was a purser in the British Merchant Navy.

Mason Gladwin

His merchant marine ship was torpedoed, and the doors became jammed. His brother, who was in the boiler room with him, and other crewmembers could not escape from the ship. Mason and the others, who had not burned alive on the ship, were taken to the hospital to be treated for severe third degree burns over their entire bodies. Mason barely survived and suffered miserably for about two weeks before passing away.

Sometime after that she met Alfred McWhirter, who ended up being her second husband until he passed away in November of 1961. Molly never remarried after that; perhaps losing two husbands is a little strenuous on an individual.

April 1, 2010
Thursday

I am working on vocabulary words, and I'm slightly confused. I came across the word "cadaver." I know what that means, but right underneath it, it says, "cadaverous/adj." How do you even use that in a sentence?

He had a cadaverous look on his face.

You are so cadaverous when we make love.

It just doesn't seem correct to me. Shows what I know.

Molly and I had another talk about Grandma June today. Molly was telling about when she found out she was pregnant, and one of the first things she remembers worrying about was what to name the child. She doesn't remember what the name choices were if it happened to be a boy, but she ended up naming my grandma after the month she was born in, June. I guess that makes sense, but I never realized it before today. I guess it would be a little strange to be named June and have a birthday in October. I wonder if that is the same for most people who are named after months? I never made that association before. June is the only person

I can think of, whom I know personally, who is named after a month.

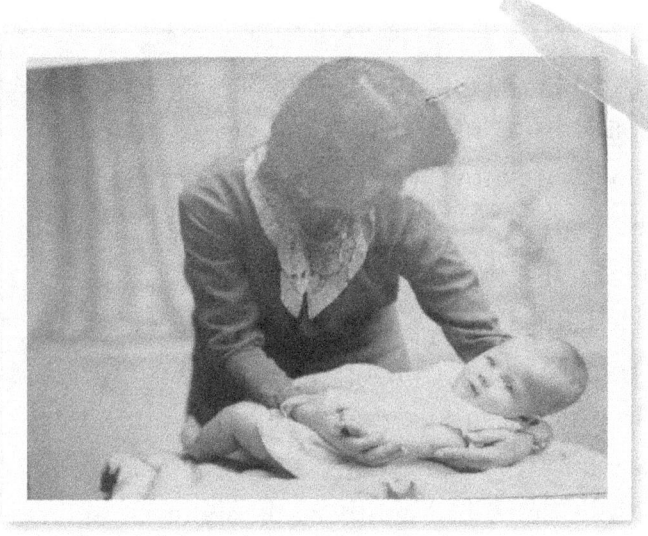

Molly and June

~Minerva

April 3, 2010
Saturday

Today has been very weird for me. Early this morning right around three o'clock, I woke up to the sound of two people talking. At first I thought it was Molly's neighbor, Jerry. I thought maybe he was watching Roseanne again. He likes to do that at stupid o'clock—just about every morning.

I sat up so I could hear a bit better. It was at that point I realized it wasn't coming from Jerry's direction, but rather, it was coming from Molly's room. She giggled, and it freaked me out. I could hear a man's voice, but I couldn't make out what he was saying. The whole scenario was completely irrational, and it didn't make sense to me. I knew there is no one in there with her.

Now, I am wide-awake and trying to rationalize what I'm hearing. I get out of bed and slowly walk over to the edge of the living room. At this point I am standing about three feet from Molly's bedroom door. I hear her say, "No, I didn't know Sunday is Easter."

Then I hear the man's voice saying something else, but I can't make it out because it's almost as if he has his hand up over his mouth. It reminded me of that SNL skit with the people talking all muffled. I think it was with Chris Kattan. It was a funny skit. Not funny at the present time, though. Then I hear Molly say, "No, I won't forget." Then there is a pause for a few seconds before she starts in again.

"When are you coming to visit again?" I hear the man's muffled voice again. I am straining so hard to hear what he is saying. I'm squinting my eyes, as if that is going to help with my hearing. I'm so weirded out and so intrigued at the same time. I take a step closer to her door. It's pitch black because the nightlight was not on for some reason. I'm trying to be extremely quiet and not make any noise. I hear Molly again, "Well, when do I get to come be with you?" The question was just bizarre to begin with. The muffled voice sounded so familiar. If I could just catch a clear word or phrase, it would cue my memory. And then it hit me all at once: I recognized the voice. I was having trouble placing the voice at first because I hadn't heard it in almost twenty-five years.

It was my father's voice, unmistakably and undeniably. I immediately got goose bumps.

I did not know what to do. Facts at that specific moment in time included the following:

1. My father died in 1988.
2. Grandma was, or believed she was, having a conversation with someone.
3. I was, or believed I was, listening to my deceased father's voice. I listened so intently. I wanted to hear what he was saying more than anything in the whole world. I could hear Molly's voice, crystal-clear, just as she could apparently hear his. Then I heard her say, "Before my birthday?" There was a short muffled response from my father's voice. "Well, what day?" I heard another muffled response from my father's voice.

"Well, when will you know?" I heard another muffled response from my father's voice. I could not handle it any longer. I took the two more steps to Molly's bedroom door and flipped on the light really quickly.

"Hey, Grandma!" I said all excitedly.

"Hello, dear." She looked surprised and was looking around the room.

"Who are you talking to, Grandma?" She was shaking her head and sporting a smile on her face, almost like she knows I'm not going to believe her. She kind of mouths the word "nah" a few times while shaking her head—still smiling.

"I heard you talking to someone, Grandma—who was it?" I'm hoping she will answer me. I don't know what answer I was expecting honestly. Something rational, I guess.

"My grandson." Her answer was simple, to the point, and completely surreal. I got chills all over my body.

"Were you talking to Rocky again?" At that point, I was trying to see if she knows whom she is talking about.

"No," she smiles and points to the picture on the wall, right above the light switch, by which I am standing several inches away from. "My grandson, Dave. Do you know him?" I was straight up not being able to handle the unexplainable.

"Yes, Grandma, I know him. I have to go to the bathroom. Good night!" I shut off the light, took a piss, and then I stayed awake in bed for the rest of the morning. I hate not being able to have a rational explanation for things—it's just weird. I don't know why it creeps me out so bad. I am open to believing anything; I just need an explanation, and I haven't got one for this yet.

~*Minerva*

April 19, 2010
Monday

Grandma and I had an awesome conversation today. I am sure if placed into action, it may be considered illegal in most states. I blame Molly because she started the whole topic of conversation. While eating breakfast this morning she told me that I am not allowed to cry after she passes away. That coming from her mouth was somewhat shocking. I immediately thought today might be the day; I thought maybe she was just prepping me to be kind. I told her I might not be able to control myself because I will be sad.

She then informed me that after she passes away, she would still be able to see me. I must have looked surprised; her comment was shocking. I asked her to elaborate on that; I told her that I thought the rule was once someone is dead, that's it. I told her I didn't think for example that after she passed away, she would be able to look down on me and make sure I was behaving properly for the rest of my life. She proceeded to inform me I was wrong.

Molly explained to me that after she dies, she, or her sprit, or her soul, or some piece of her, will float above the whole world. She believes she will be able to see what is going on. I asked a couple questions for clarification purposes. I definitely did not want to misinterpret what she was telling me. Basically after she dies, she believes a piece of her remains on this earth so she can watch over all of us. I asked her if she would be watching me after she passes away, and she said most definitely.

Then for some unknown reason I got a ridiculous idea in my head. Since we were already having a theoretical and hypothetical conversation, I shared my thoughts. With the preface of knowing Molly loves riding in the Chevelle, I asked her the following question. Since she already knew that her soul would be sticking around after she died, I asked her if she would like me to take her for a ride in the Chevelle after she passed away. She said it sounded like fun. We came to the conclusion that after she passes away, I should take her body down to the Chevelle and go for one last drive around town. She thinks that if her body is there, she will be able to remember and experience the ride as a soul. I cannot understand the reasoning behind her thought and I cannot decide if the idea of driving around with my dead great-grandmother is sweet, creepy, or bizarre.

~Minerva

"That which you do not know——you
wish to know; and what you do not
know——you never use."

~*Brewer*

"There is a day before me and night
behind me. To live happily between
is the key to happiness."
"My life——so hard to rate it;
It's meaning——I do translate It."

~*Brewer*

Molly and I took a shower sitting down today for the first time. She was complaining on Sunday when we bathed, saying she didn't want to stand up anymore. I am all for whatever makes her comfortable. I called June on Sunday and told her we needed to look into getting a stool/seat for the shower, so I can have Molly sit down and then help her bathe.

Today I used a chair from her utility closet that I knew was in there. It is a metal/hard plastic chicken wire type chair that I normally see out in people's lawns. I placed a couple towels on the seat so it would be soft and comfy when she sat down, and I placed a couple against the back of the chair so she could lean against the back of the chair and be comfortable. The shower worked out great, and she liked sitting down very much.

I have also noticed that Molly is getting more confused when I ask her to pick out an outfit for the day. So today I picked one out for her and laid it out on the bed, which is what I normally do. The only difference is that I didn't ask her to select the outfit of choice.

She had no problem getting dressed once I helped her get the adult diapers pulled up around her waist. They are a snug fit, so she needs assistance with those. Besides that minor detail, she puts her pants on by herself, and still puts her undershirt and button up shirt on with no help from me. The buttons are frustrating her more, but she loves to wear the button up shirts. So I just ask her if I can help her with the buttons and she smiles and nods her head. I put her socks on and she comes out to the living room for tea.

Whenever we decide to take a walk, or whenever we decide to step out for a few, I put her shoes on for her. I always ask her if I can help her with her shoes, and she always smiles and thanks me for my assistance. Her shoes are extremely comfortable, but they are tie shoes, so she cannot bend over and tie them any longer, which is totally reasonable. I have no problem tying her shoes; that is what I am there for.

I woke up to Molly on the floor again this morning. My main goal is to keep the confusion, agitation, and aggression to a minimum. I understand that Molly may be having a difficult time communicating with me. I know that the hallucinations and delusions are classic symptoms of an individual with Alzheimer's, but experiencing this first hand is something I never imagined. Luckily Molly does not get agitated very often because I mold the environment and bend reality around her. I have found her on the floor a couple times now, and my biggest concern is bone fractures and pain of any kind. My first assessment and main priority is her comfort.

I asked her this morning if she was in any pain, and she said no. It is somewhat frustrating for me because I don't know if she is being truthful and is not in pain, or if she is in pain and doesn't realize it. Luckily the few times I have found her on the floor it is in the morning when we would be getting up to get dressed anyway. She is very happy to wrap her arms around me and trusts me to pick her up at this point. That is a monumental step from when I first moved in with her. This morning I helped her get dressed and put lotion on her while assessing for any broken bones. She told me she got down on the floor to hide from the men. It was another delusion that I played along with and was happy she was not injured. After getting dressed and having some breakfast, we went down to the common room so I could play the piano for Molly while she happily enjoyed tea and biscuits.

~Minerva

April 22, 2010
Thursday

Phosphenes – that is the word of the day. Molly sees them everywhere. I am not sure if she had noticed them before – but today was the first time I've ever seen her grab at them.

I asked her what she was doing and what she was looking at. She described the spaghetti shape, worm-looking creatures to me. She said she kept seeing them float by and she asked if I could see them. I told her I could see them – which is true to an extent…if I close my eyes or stare at the wall – I will see phosphenes from time to time.

It is pretty funny, Molly will be sitting there in her chair, and then she just reaches out into the air and tries to grab hold of the phosphene – which she doesn't realize at this point, can never be caught.

I know I always hear Molly when and if she gets up in the middle of the night. This morning was the first time I saw her head for the front door with her walker and coat on. I saw her attempting to unlock the door, and I jumped up and walked over to her. I asked her if she was going somewhere and she said down to check the mail. I told her it might be a good idea if we both get dressed first. I told her I forgot to get dressed and she looked at me in my t-shirt and panties and informed me I could not go down to the mailbox looking as if something reminiscent of what the cat would drag in. I suggested we both get dressed and then go down to check the mail, and that is exactly what we did. I am going to start wedging the doorstopper under the front door. I know she can't figure that out, and I know she is not strong enough to move it. Several times it has been there, and she has asked me to move it for her.

I feel very lucky that Molly is who she is, because I can handle her by myself. She is about five feet tall and weighs in at about ninety pounds. I know not everyone who is taking care of a family member is as lucky or as fortunate as I am. I am in my early thirties and lifting Molly is not an issue for me. Bathing her and helping her dress does not tire me out. The hallucinations, delusions, and other behavioral changes are quite tolerable because I understand on a basic level how Alzheimer's works and progresses. I know that if I needed help or assistance, my bother would come help me. It is reassuring to know that I have support as well. As Molly's condition worsens, I can feel myself getting sadder. I am sad because I know what is to come. So I focus on the positives and remember how lucky Molly and I both are. She is in amazing health and has no medications to take. She still walks with her walker and is quite independent in most cases. Although the decline is obvious to me, I wonder if she realizes what is happening to her. I would be so depressed if roles were reversed and I could comprehend what was happening. I really hope for the sake of Molly's happiness that she is oblivious to the progression of the Alzheimer's. She always seems so happy and cheerful; I think that is a sincere feeling, and I really hope it is because I successfully help her feel safe, secure, and reassured.

~Jaime

April 25, 2010
Sunday

Molly woke me up about two o'clock this morning—she said she wanted some tea and biscuits. So I helped her out of bed, and we made our way to her comfy chair by the window. I made us both a cup of tea, and we visited. She ate four coconut biscuits, one regular biscuit, and two Apple Newton thingies.

By the time three thirty rolled around, Molly was tired and ready for bed again. We got her sorted out, and then I fell asleep out on my bed. I had a dream about shopping for biscuits—how lame.

I was on the search for vanilla cream biscuits, and every store I went to was out of stock. I tried Albertson's and Fred Meyer's. I tried Wal-Mart and Shopko. I tried WinCo and Costco. The dream was exhausting. It was literally hours of looking for some cookies. I remember songs playing on the car radio as I drove from store to store. I remember sitting at red lights.

I remember driving past Big Bun and wondering why the line was so long. What a bizarre dream. I am the biscuit hunter.

~Nicks

April 30, 2010
Friday

I had to carry Molly down to June's car today. She did not want to walk, and she said she never wanted her hair done again; she had decided she doesn't like going to get her hair done.

I kept her distracted by talking about tea and biscuits. I told her I would fix her the best cup of tea in the world, once we had arrived at the beauty school and got her hair washed. She liked that idea. I told her I would not make her get her hair done ever again if she would just agree to go with me. I told her June would get worried and concerned if we didn't show up, and I told her we would have to pay for the services even if we didn't show up. So she agreed to have her hair done one more time, and I vowed to never take her to the hair salon again. I told June today that I was keeping that promise. She is now worried about how Molly will get her hair washed and set, and I told her we can find a girl to come to the house and do it in the living room.

I was entertaining Molly and myself by asking random and ludicrous questions while driving to the salon like these:

1. Do you think that zebras should keep the stripes, or should they switch to spots, like the leopard?
2. Were you a fan of Hitler's work?
3. Mayonnaise – do we need it?

She was laughing and having a great time by the time we arrived at the beauty school. While she was getting her hair washed, I made her a cup of tea and pulled out a few biscuits for her that I had brought from home.

~Minerva

May 2, 2010
Sunday

Molly and I talked about Jackpot, Nevada today. She wants to go—but she does not want to hang out with Harry Potter. She has convinced herself Harry Potter will be on the bus, and he will steal all the toilet paper. I am almost to the point of being convinced that if we ride the fun bus down to Jackpot, Harry Potter will be on it. Oh, my goodness, that is so funny.

She keeps talking about the free alcohol, and how she can't wait to take advantage of that. I asked her if she wanted a shot of whisky or vodka. She said whisky. I might have to make a special little trip to the liquor store.

Molly was telling me about how she used to ride the bus down to Jackpot and stay over night or do a turn-around. The turn around apparently means you head to Jackpot around six or seven o'clock in the morning, get there around ten, play all day, then get back on the bus around five or six in the evening, and head back to Boise.

Molly was telling me about how much fun she had on the bus and in Jackpot. I asked her if we should ride the bus or drive June's car. She said she wants to take June's car, so we don't run into Harry Potter.

So now I am thinking we might have to plan a little trip to the fabulous town of Jackpot, Nevada, population: 142.

~Jaime

May 3, 2010
Monday

Oh, my goodness—Molly had me up most of the night. About one thirty in the morning, she wakes up and tells me she is hungry. So great—I get up and help her get dressed. We head out to the living room and she let me know she wanted to sit at the kitchen table this time, rather than her comfy chair over by the window. I asked her if she would like some soup, and she said yes.

I opened a can of chicken noodle and heated up a small portion for her. I put the bowl in front of her, and she asked me what was in the bowl. I told her it was the chicken noodle soup. She shakes her head in disgust and tells me she does not want it. I take it away from the table and ask her what sounds good to her.

She told me she wanted cereal. I asked her if she wanted a bowl of Raisin Bran, and she told me she did. So I fixed her a bowl of raisin bran—her favorite—and place it in front of her. She stares at it for about thirty seconds and then asks me what is in the bowl. I tell her it's the raisin bran she had requested. She makes another disgusted face, and tells me she does not want it. I started laughing at this point.

I realized at this point that some major hardwiring connections are being crossed. Molly asks me for something, and then minutes later, she does not remember asking me. The whole scenario is quite intriguing. I asked her again if she was hungry. She told me she was starving and she wanted a pot pie because it sounded so tasty. I asked her if she was sure she wanted a pot pie, and she re-confirmed her request for a beef pot pie. I make her a beef pot pie—yummy, yum, yum—and I place it in front of her. Do you want to guess what happened next?

She looked at if for a minute, then picked up her spoon. I felt so glorious and victorious inside. I had finally put something in front of her that she truly wanted to eat. Then came the surprise ending. With her spoon in hand, she asked me what I had put in front of her. I told her it was a delicious Marie Callender's beef pot pie. She looked at with a hateful stare of discontent and told me she did not want it.

We ended up eating coconut biscuits and having a couple cups of tea. The short-circuiting that is taking place in her brain is very interesting.

It doesn't hurt her physically, but it is occurring more and more frequently. As long as I can distract her and keep her from feeling confused or embarrassed, she seems to be fantastic.

Side note. This morning around ten o'clock, Molly said she wanted to take a nap. I left her in her favorite chair; she was watching traffic out the window. I was working on a painting on the floor for about half an hour and then got up to make a cup of tea. I checked on Molly, and she looked strange. Something was not right. It was like she was staring out the window, but her eyes weren't moving. My heart immediately dropped, and I thought she had passed away. Her eyes were open, and I waved my hand in front of her face. She was completely non-responsive, but when I looked at her chest she was breathing. I clapped my hands in front of her face; she blinked, and snapped out of it.

I asked her if she was okay. She said yes and told me she was just zoning out and listening to the traffic outside. I was wondering if she had a stroke or mini-seizure of some sort, but she sounded so convincing that everything was okay. She claimed that she knew I was there working on my painting and claims she saw me get up and stand in front of her for the few seconds that I did. So I left it alone. I just thought the incident was interesting to note.

~*James*

May 4, 2010
Tuesday

Today was rough. Molly woke up about nine o'clock, and she seemed very angry. She said she did not want to eat breakfast. I told her that was fine, and I told her she could let me know when she was hungry.

She also informed me she was not getting dressed for the day. I asked her if she had a good reason for not wanting to get dressed. She told me she didn't feel like it. She said she didn't understand why we had to get dressed every day if at the end of each day we got back into our nightgowns. I could see the point being valid, and I told her that.

I also told her getting dressed might make her feel a bit better. I told her we never know who is going to stop by. That usually does the trick, because for some reason, she does not want to answer the door in her nightgown.

After getting her dressed, we made our way out into the living room, and I helped her sit at the kitchen table. I asked her if she wanted some tea, and she said no. For the first time I think in ninety- some-odd years, she declined tea. I knew she was either not feeling well, or it was getting close to that inevitable time. The vacant stares, not wanting to get dressed at any point, and the loss of appetite for food or tea seemed to be classic signs the Grim Reaper is near.

Molly did not want to sit in her chair for some reason. I asked her if she wanted to go downstairs with me, and she agreed. Good deal. I thought if I could get her out of the apartment, I could entertain her downstairs with some piano playing and people watching. I can't think of a better way to spend my late morning or early afternoon.

Grandma said she couldn't walk. So I picked her up, and she put her arms around me. She completely trusts me.

I remember what happened when I first moved in here. Shortly after my move-in date, she fell down, and I had to pick her up for the first time. When I was picking her up, she was scared I was going to drop her. I told her as long as she was not kicking and screaming everything would be fine. She seemed to always remember that.

She held on tight, and I carried her down the hallway to the elevator. I told her she would have to push the button, and she did a splendid job of selecting the down arrow button without any prompts from me.

We got downstairs, and I carried her across the hallway and into the common room where I sat her in her favorite spot. I played the piano for about fifteen minutes and then sat with her on the couch, making comments about the people who would pass by us. After about half an hour, she wanted to go back upstairs. So I picked her up, and we headed to the elevators. We rode up to her floor and headed on down the hallway, back to her apartment.

Molly did not want to sit in her recliner chair by the window. I offered the wheel chair we had gotten for her, and she agreed to sit in that. I got one of the pillows off her bed and sat it on the seat first. When I sat her in the wheel chair, she smiled. I asked her if she was comfortable, and she told me she was. I finally got her to eat a few bites of chocolate pudding, so I guess that is better than nothing.

The day was tough. I kept trying to get Molly to move, and she didn't want to. I tried to get her to go to the couch, and she wouldn't have anything to do with it. I also tried to get her to sit in her favorite chair of all time. She was not having anything to do with that either. She pretty much stayed in the wheelchair all day: doing nothing, drinking nothing, and eating nothing. She finally asked if she could get into bed about four in the afternoon, and I told her that was fine. I carried her to the bedroom, I put her nightgown on, and I placed her into bed. She held my hand for a few minutes and told me she appreciated everything I had done for her. She was creeping me out. I told her I would see her in the morning, and she smiled. I kissed her on her forehead and left her to sleep.

I did check on her about six o'clock. When I went to the bathroom I couldn't help but look in to make sure she was okay. Her eyes were open, and she was staring at the ceiling. I asked her if she was okay, and she was unresponsive again. I walked over to her, waved my hand in front of her face, and she came to. She told me she was thinking about where she is going, and how she wants to get there.

~*Nicks*

May 5, 2010
Wednesday

Things are continuing to go downhill at this point. I informed June this morning of Molly's well-being status. She said she would be by shortly to visit and spend some time with us. Molly did not want to get out of bed this morning until I told her June was coming by. She became so angry at the fact she had to get up and get dressed. I tried not to show the smile on my face. We put on her favorite pink and gold outfit; it consists of rose-colored slacks and a nice button-down, gold-colored shirt with roses on it. Molly looked beautiful, as she always does. She was craving chocolate pudding again. Someone please remind me to write Bill Cosby when I get a free moment and thank him for providing the only nutritional supplement my great-grandmother would tolerate.

After the delicious and nutritious chocolate pudding breakfast, sponsored by Jell-O®, Molly and I enjoyed a cup of tea. She was still refusing to sit in her recliner by the window, which I cannot for the life of me figure out. She enjoyed sitting in the wheelchair with the pillow, which reminded me of one of those booster seats I used to sit in at Pizza Hut® as a child. Molly refused to walk anywhere, so I carried her to the bathroom when she said she needed to go, and then I brought her back to the wheelchair.

Today for the first time, Molly lost control of her bowels. I am unsure if it was a one-time thing, or if this is something I can expect from now on. The harsh reality of life, combined with my intuition, tells me the time is winding down for Molly. Again, I am unsure if the incontinence is a permanent thing in cases like these.

I carried Molly into the bathroom and asked her to please stand and hang on to the rails while I got her soiled clothes off of her. She apologized several times, stating she didn't understand what had happened. I reassured her everything was okay and would be okay. I told her she had had an accident but backed it up with the comment that we all have them from time to time. I told her I did the same thing the day before. She smiled at me and looked more at ease about the situation. After getting her cleaned up, I carried her into her bedroom. The bedroom was a clean place for her to sit while I cleaned up the bathroom, living room, and wheelchair.

Molly and I had a great talk while I was cleaning the bathroom, and she was sitting across the hall on her bed. We were discussing June, and how Molly was proud of her as a mother and grandmother. Molly told me she was not keen on having a child to begin with, but over time, June changed her mind. In the context of the dynamics between my grandmother and my great-grandmother, this was an amazing statement for Molly to make.

I kept thinking that I would be so lucky to live a fun and full life as my great-grandmother had. She was living proof and the perfect example of how I wanted my life to go. Not necessarily with the choices that she had made but with her attitude and motivations.

I believe that Molly made it this far because of her attitude on life. She has always had a great outlook on life and she is always preaching about how every day is a gift. Molly takes no medications and is never in pain. That is how I want to be: healthy and happy. So far, so good.

June made it over around eleven, and the three of us enjoyed a cup of tea. Molly made the decision to sit in her recliner, which she has been so reluctant to sit in for the past couple days. I am not sure if it was the fact June was coming by—if that was the motivating factor—but I am stumped.

I could tell June saw a difference in Molly. She is moving a great deal slower, even though her cognitive thoughts seem to be functioning spectacularly. I saw the sadness in June's eyes, and I made a mental note to comfort her later and remind her of the positive aspects that I had been reflecting on while cleaning up in the bathroom.

June stayed for about half an hour and then took off. Molly asked if she could take a nap, and I told her she could do anything she wanted to do, as long as we agreed to plan the Jackpot trip soon.

She smiled that smile that I know all too well. It is the look that says, "Dear child, I understand what you are doing, and I appreciate your noble efforts to keep me focused on the distractions."

I let Molly sleep for about an hour, and I could hear her snoring; it was not loud and obnoxious but rather a comforting sound that reassured me she was still in the game.

When I went to wake her up a little after noon, she told me she would be up in just a few minutes. After a few minutes, I heard no rustling around or calls for me to go in and pick her up, so I went in to check on her. Again with the non-responsive routine, I had to check on her to make sure she was still breathing. She was. I waved my hand in front of her face and then snapped my fingers. She blinked, and her eyes dilated.

I asked her if she was okay, and she nodded her head, yes. I asked her if she would like to come out and visit with me for a while because I was lonely. She agreed. She sat in her wheelchair, and I gave her a manicure and pedicure.

We chatted about how she did not like going to the salon to get her hair done. I told her we should definitely talk to June about arranging something else—like me doing her hair at home. She thought that was a splendid idea.

If this idea gets approved, I hope I don't end up making her look like Bozo the Clown. Doing her hair might be the end of me, but I would never let her know that. I am all for doing and saying whatever it takes to keep Molly content and happy. That is what she deserves.

Molly decided bedtime was about four o'clock again, so I carried her into the bedroom, got her into her nightgown, and then situated her in bed so she was comfortable. She held my hand again and told me I was wonderful. I told her she might be delirious. She laughed and then informed me that she was completely coherent during our conversation, and she knew exactly what she was talking about.

She didn't have to convince me, I believed her.

~James

May 6, 2010
Tuesday

Today started out with a miracle: Molly wanted to eat two pudding cups for breakfast and drink some water. I had told her last night before she went to sleep that a visit to the doctor's office may be in order if she didn't want to start eating a little bit more than one pudding cup a day and not consuming any water. I am hoping the idea stuck; whether consciously or subconsciously, it doesn't matter to me. After breakfast, I told her I was going to run to the store to grab a few things and asked her if she wanted to go. I was hoping I could get her out of the apartment for a little bit.

She said she most certainly did not want to go, and on top of that, she requested that I not go either. She asked me to please stay with her all day, and I immediately agreed.

I didn't know if she felt different, or if she knew something I didn't know. The way she asked me to stay with her though was powerful; it was as if nothing else mattered for the rest of the day. I stayed right by her side and held her hand for the majority of the day, minus when I went to the bathroom or entered the kitchen to make us a cup of tea. As long as she could see me, she was fine. So today I went to the bathroom all day with the door open so Molly could see me. She would wave and smile, and in return I, too, waved and smiled while urinating.

We talked about Jackpot and making reservations. I asked her if we could share a room to save some money. She told me about the time she worked at a hotel in Salt Lake City and the Beatles were touring through town. She told me about how a couple of them had flirted with her while they were staying there. She was invited upstairs to their hotel room when she got off work. She said they hung out for a couple hours and laughed about comparing Yanks to Brits. Being they were all from the same neck of the woods, it makes sense they had some common grounds on which to feel comfortable.

Molly wanted to go to bed around four in the afternoon again, so I helped get her nightgown on and get situated in bed. She asked me to stay with her, and she grabbed my hand. I sat down on the side of the bed with her and told her I would stay with her and hold her hand until she went to sleep. She asked me to stay with her all night, and

I knew something was up. She was clingy all day as if she knew something or could feel something going on with her body.

I went and got her wheelchair and pulled it right next to her side of the bed so I could reach her hand. I wrapped myself in my blanket, got comfortable, and held her hand. I watched her looking around at the ceiling, almost as if she was able to hear something upstairs that I could not. After about half an hour, she fell asleep. The way her hand slowly stopped grasping mine was very strange. It felt as if she was slipping away, and I thought for sure she would not make it through the night.

I lay awake for an undetermined amount of time. I was thankful I didn't have to go to the bathroom, because I did not want to wake Molly up by moving my hand. I was thinking very peaceful things about Molly, and how thankful I was to be the one getting to spend so much time with her. I thought about how I was happy because Molly was constantly teaching me things. I always thought that if I was ever in a situation like the one I am now, I would be scared when the end neared.

Molly taught me that I do not know myself as well as I thought. Molly has taught me that life and death can be very beautiful experiences, and no one should be afraid of either. I sat in her wheelchair, holding her hand, smiling, and feeling very peaceful with how everything was playing out.

~James

May 7, 2010
Friday

I fell asleep late last night; I bet it had to be around four or five in the morning. Molly woke me up when she moved her hand, and when I looked over at the clock, it was almost eight. She told me she had to go to the bathroom, so I jumped up and moved the wheelchair out of the way. My back was so sore from sleeping in the position I did.

I took Molly to the bathroom, and she was mumbling something about the toilet paper. I asked her what she was talking about, and if she wanted to share her thoughts. She told me she was tired of Harry Potter sneaking into her apartment at night and stealing her toilet paper.

Back to the Harry Potter story line. I was astonished that she even remembered his name, or the fact I told her he was stealing toilet paper. Perhaps I have underestimated how precious of a commodity Molly's toilet paper is to her. I had to smile because I thought to myself, "My great-grandmother cannot remember a long-term memory like who I am but has made damn sure to permanently tattoo the image of Harry Potter stealing her toilet paper into her mind." I don't care who you are—you have to laugh at that. That is hilarious, and I will never forget the Harry Potter toilet paper scandal for as long as I live.

I told Molly we had won an unlimited supply of toilet paper from Albertson's. She did not seem impressed. I told her now that we have unlimited supplies of the stuff, we should be a little more lenient on Harry Potter, because perhaps he is not as fortunate as we are. She replied, "Why is Albertson's giving us toilet paper?"

I responded, "Because it's your store, Grandma."

She seemed very insulted by what I had said and replied, "It is not my store." She said that with a very disgusted tone to her voice. I was trying not to laugh; she obviously didn't remember the jingle that sometimes plays on television for Albertson's. I am pretty sure the phrase, "Albertson's, it's your store," is their motto. I told her I had entered the 2010 toilet paper sweepstakes and had won. Then she seemed pretty happy about the whole ordeal. She said the idea of free toilet paper wasn't such a bad idea.

After I got her out of the bathroom, we had some tea and pudding. I had promised her back about three or four days ago, that for every pudding cup she ate, I would match her. I never told her that I don't like chocolate to begin with. Anyone who knows me knows I would take vanilla over chocolate any day of the week. But I reluctantly swallowed my pride and the pudding. Molly ate two pudding cups today. I love that this is all she wants to eat now. It wouldn't matter if all she wanted was Alaskan king crab, I would make sure she had it.

I reminded Molly it was Friday, which was go-get-our-hair-done day. The good mood disappeared instantaneously. I told her it was a fabulous Friday, because we weren't going to the hair salon.

I reminded her that I had promised the week before that we would never go to the salon again. She told me she wanted to sit in her recliner and enjoy a cup of tea, while looking out the window. I carried her from her wheelchair to her recliner and then went in the kitchen and made us both a cup of tea. I was thinking about how Molly has not walked anywhere for the past week or so; it has been me carrying her everywhere. I was wondering if she is too weak to stand at this point. I'm also wondering if that is why she threw a hissy about not wanting to get her hair done today. She does not like to be seen in public with me carrying her. She likes the strong, independent façade she thinks everyone falls for. Whatever makes her happy though, and at that moment, she was happy.

I held Molly's hand for a bit while we watched people and traffic outside. I asked her if I could go visit Grandma June about ten thirty, since she would be at the hair salon by herself. She patted my hand, smiled at me, nodded her head, and told me I was a good kid. The plan was to meet June, as she was finishing up her appointment. We were going to get the flowers for Molly and head back here to the apartment. It was only about half past nine in the morning so Molly and I started to chat. I asked her how she was feeling today. She said today was a good day for her to go. I immediately started thinking of places she wanted to go; obviously the hair salon was not one of them. Then she continued on explaining she was tired and exhausted. It was at that point the sharp blade of reality cut me. I asked her if I could get her anything. She said she just wanted me to hold her hand and visit with her for a while. The way she held my hand was different; as if there was no strength left in her. I was holding her hand in mine and asked her on a scale of one to ten, how happy she was that we weren't going to the hair salon today. She smiled and squeezed my hand. She turned and looked out the window; I could see her watching traffic at the corner.

We watched the traffic for a few minutes until her hand started to slip out of mine. I leaned forward a bit so I could see her face better; I noticed she wasn't blinking. I squeezed her hand a little, and addressed her. "Grandma?" There was no reply. I started to get tears in my eyes as the harsh reality began to set in. I stood up and stuck my face in front of hers. "Hey Grandma, guess what?" Again, she did not answer. I immediately thought about our conversation we had, discussing the fact she would still be around in spirit after she died. I felt half a smile on my face while actually contemplating and entertaining the idea of taking grandma Molly's corpse down to the Chevelle and taking her for one last ride around town. After a few moments my heart sank. I thought, "Why today?" I had just got off the phone with June and we had planned to get flowers later this afternoon for Mother's day and come back to the apartment.

I knew June was at the salon at that particular moment in time, getting her hair done. I couldn't build up the nerve or courage to call her and explain to her that her mother passed away. All I could think about was the fact I didn't want to break the news to June on the phone, while she had rollers in her hair. The stupid things I think about. I put my fingers on Molly's wrist, attempting and partially expecting to find a pulse; there was nothing. The complete stillness and serenity of her body reconfirmed my thought; she was gone. I closed her eyes and looked at my phone; it was 9:52 and I couldn't think. I couldn't breathe. I was sad and happy at the same time. Sad Molly had passed away before June was able to come see her, but very thankful she passed away so peacefully.

I thought Molly's passing would be the most difficult part of this whole experience but I never took into account the aftermath. Now I had to tell June. I guess I had never thought this far ahead; I was completely filled with anxiety and stress. It seems I had just talked to June moments before and we had a game plan so she could bring her mother flowers for Mother's day. That game plan is now permanently tainted with death; there is no happy ending with this scenario. I kissed grandma Molly on the forehead and left her in the apartment.

I don't remember walking down to the car or driving to the hair salon; I only remember trying to figure out a way to tell grandma June what had happened. I remember arriving at the salon and checking my face in the review mirror. I hadn't been crying since I left Molly's, so I looked okay. I had never felt more anxious in my entire life. I walked up to the salon doors and opened them. I put on a game face and walked around until I found June; she was almost done with her appointment. The girl who does June's hair was brushing it out. I didn't want June asking me about Molly, so I continued asking her random questions. I commented on her hair looking fabulous and asked her what kind of flowers she had in mind for Molly. She said we could look around at Albertson's because they normally have quite an impressive selection to choose from. I told her I was going to get a cup of coffee and asked her if she wanted one; she did not. I walked over to the coffee machine area and took my time making a cup of coffee. I put in four packets of that nasty powdered creamer, and I took my sweet time opening and dispersing each packet.

When I got back to where June was sitting, she was just getting up and putting her coat on. We walked up front to pay for the hair-do and then we walked down to Albertsons. I didn't say anything about anything. I couldn't. June and I grabbed a pretty bouquet and headed back to Molly's.

I unlocked the door and peaked in to see Molly lying unresponsive in the chair. It was the same unresponsive position I had left her in when I went to go visit June. I didn't want June to see her mother in the unresponsive state; I knew it would upset her. I told her just to hang on a minute while I went and woke up Molly. June asked me if everything was okay and I reassured her it was.

The entire time I was focused on Molly, I could simultaneously hear Grandma June behind me. At first she was fussing and wrestling about with the flowers in the kitchen, and then she came in the living room and was saying things like, "No. Really? Are you sure?"

I told her to go ahead and call the coroner, and I would move Molly into the bedroom so June would not be forced to look at or be in the same room with her dead mother. I gently picked up Molly, and I remember thinking it was so weird that she wasn't wrapping her arms around me to hold me tight, like she had done so many times before. I started to get teary-eyed as I passed June and made my way into the bedroom. I remember telling myself that I couldn't cry just yet, because I didn't want to breakdown in front of June. I didn't want to make things worse for her.

I placed Molly gently on the bed and placed her arms at her side. Her eyes had slightly opened again, so I closed them. Her mouth had opened as well, so I closed it and tried to make her look as comfortable as possible.

Thinking back, that was a strange thing for me to do; technically, I don't think Molly would have been uncomfortable in any position I placed her in. It was more of a respect thing to me. I thought about how she was, and how she liked to be presentable whenever company came by. So that is what I was doing—making sure she was presentable for her last visitors. I stood there looking at Molly. I made the decision to not tell June about Molly passing away that morning before I came to see her at the salon. I don't know if I was justifying or rationalizing why I withheld the information about the exact time when Molly had died. Either way, what would it change?

I closed the door and went out into the living room to wait with June. I opened the window because it felt really hot in there. June said I could turn on the fan. I told her that might not be a bad idea to circulate the air, and I didn't think Molly would mind either. Grandma smiled at me. Leave it to me to have the world's toughest defense mechanisms. I don't know if humor is always appropriate, but it sure does make me feel better. The coroner came and spent about ten minutes in the room with Molly. He said it was standard protocol. The funeral home people arrived about an hour later to pick up Molly; they took her to be cremated. June and I made an appointment to head over to the funeral home the next day to sort out details.

~James

Epilogue

As I sit and reflect on everything Molly taught me, I wear a huge smile. Molly taught me so much about individuals who progress through the stages of Alzheimer's. I could have read fifty psychology books on Alzheimer's and never learned a fraction of what I did while living with Molly. She reminded me that the mind is a very fragile piece of life, not to be taken for granted.

She also reminded me of some very valuable lessons. I am reminded to keep a sense of humor. I hope I can laugh as much as Molly did; her sense of humor was amazing. I noticed that we laughed at all the same jokes, so I think I am in good shape. I am also reminded not to take life so seriously. I tend to follow Henry David Thoreau's simplistic approach to life.

Most importantly, Molly taught me to accept the things I cannot change. If I ever get to the point where my memory starts to give in and fade, I hope I can accept reality with honor and dignity. If I ever get to the point where I need help with anything, I hope I have the strength and humility to ask for assistance. Remembering that every day could be my last is a very important thought for me. It reminds me to never take anything for granted and regret nothing.

Molly passed away in May of 2010 and I did not have the opportunity to take her ashes up to Canada until September of 2011. Regardless of the time that passed, I kept my promise to Molly. I snuck some of her ashes across the Canadian border and buried her with her husband in Hamilton, Ontario, Canada.

I arrived in Hamilton, Ontario about five in the afternoon. Fairly quickly, I located the tombstone of Molly's husband. I placed the flowers along the top of the tombstone; they fit nicely. I pulled out my little trowel shovel and began to dig a spot on the right side of the tombstone. The plan was to dig down deep enough so I could plant a miniature rosebush. I figured I could place the ashes in the bottom of the hole before I planted the rosebush.

The tombstone reads:
In memory of ALFRED (Mac) McWHIRTER
Apr. 25, 1915 & Nov. 26, 1961
Beloved husband of
ALICE (Molly) RADFORD
'Til we meet again'

About the Author

Minerva Nichole Spurlock is currently studying psychology and nutrition and deciding where to attend graduate school. Her passion as a writer has led to published works in literature and music.

Her broad experiences and travels across the world have taken her to over one hundred libraries, sixty countries, thirty theme parks, and five continents. She currently spends a great deal of time with her fiancé and two kitties, Sir Hercules Upchuck III and Lucktageous Pantages.